If Those Trees Could Speak

The Story of an Ascendancy Family in Ireland

by

Frank Tracy

South Dublin Libraries – March 2005

ISBN 0954766024

Design and layout by
DTP Training Unit,
The Central Remedial Clinic,
Vernon Avenue, Clontarf, Dublin 3
Phone: (01) 805 7400

Printed in Ireland by
The Central Remedial Clinic,
Vernon Avenue, Clontarf, Dublin 3

Local Studies Section
County Library
Town Centre
Tallaght
Dublin 24

Phone: 353 (0) 1 46 20073
Fax: 353 (0) 1 414 9207
e-mail: localstudies@sdublincoco.ie
web: site www.southdublin.ie

South Dublin Libraries Headquarters
Unit 1
Square Industrial Complex
Tallaght
Dublin 24

Phone: 353 (0) 1 459 7834
Fax: 353 (0) 1 459 7872

Introduction
by
Mayor Robert Dowds

South Dublin County is fortunate to have the wonderful natural resource that is Lord Massy's Woods in Killakee, within its boundaries. Anyone who takes a stroll there cannot but wonder at the wide variety of the trees, their maturity and the remains of buildings and other constructions. Most will not know of the sad tale of the "penniless peer" and of the descent of the ascendancy family associated with Killakee.

For the Sunday woodland walker or the serious historian, this book tells the story of the rise and decline of an ascendancy family. Frank Tracy has thoroughly researched the Massy family and tells their story in a lively, sympathetic way. Evocative photographs of a former age, drawn mainly from the Guinness family collection, enhance the telling of this story.

We are indebted to Frank Tracy for the effort he has put into researching and writing this fine book. Without him the full story might never have been told.

South Dublin County Council through its library service is delighted to support the study of our history and heritage by publishing this book which tells the story of part of that history and heritage and helps to explain the phenomenon that is Lord Massy's Woods.

Robert Dowds.

Robert Dowds
Mayor of South Dublin County
March 2005

CHARLES GUINNESS
(1932 -2004)

When I embarked upon my research into the family history of Lord Massy of Duntrileague I was very fortunate to meet Charles Guinness of Tibradden House, Co. Dublin. Charles was a grandson of Lucy Matilda (Massy) Guinness, daughter of the sixth Baron Massy. As a young woman Lucy Matilda Massy developed a keen interest in photography. Between 1898 and 1915 she compiled a photographic record of family life on the Massy estates at Hermitage and Killakee. Charles not only gave me access to these photographs and other Massy family memorabilia, but he also openly shared with me many anecdotes of those days as passed down to him by his parents and grandparents. Without his help and encouragement it would not have been possible to piece together many key aspects of the Massy story.

Charles Guinness was a kind, learned and thoughtful person. He also possessed a lovely, gentle sense of humour. In the short time in which I was privileged to know him we developed a warm friendship which I will always cherish.

Frank Tracy

The Author

Frank Tracy was born in the Liberties in Dublin in 1943. He was educated at James' Street CBS and University College Galway from which he graduated with a B.A. in Celtic Archaeology in 1967. He has spent most of his working life in the Public Service. A keen hillwalker and lifelong member of the scout movement, he is an active scout leader in the Merchants' Quay, Dublin scout troop. He also has a keen interest in local history and archaeology which led, among other things, to this study of the family history of Lord Massy of Duntrileague. A father of five adult children, he lives with his wife Bernie in Stillorgan, Co. Dublin.

Acknowledgements

In my pursuit of the family history of Lord Massy of Duntrileague, I was fortunate to receive information, advice and support from a great many people in Counties Dublin, Limerick, Tipperary and indeed from outside of Ireland.

I am particularly grateful to Mr Hugh Massy of Stoneville, Co Limerick, Mr Charles Guinness, Tibradden, Co. Dublin, and Mr Hugh Massy of Woodstock, Vermont USA, for sharing their records of the Massy family with me. A special word of appreciation is also due to Mr Paul Robert Massy, Leicester, England and Mrs Joan O'Kelly, Killakee, Co Dublin, for their support, advice, and encouragement. I also wish to acknowledge the assistance that I received from the staff of the National Archives, the National Library of Ireland and Trinity College Dublin Library. Finally I wish to thank Mr Oliver Doyle, Clonmel, Co. Tipperary, Mr William English, Rochestown, Co Tipperary, Mr Jim Hartigan, Castleconnell, Co. Limerick, Mr John Gallahue, Galbally, Co. Limerick and Mr Eugene Callan, Dublin, for their practical support and assistance.

A very special word of thanks is due to Michael O'Connor and the staff and trainees of the Central Remedial Clinic Desktop Publishing Unit, for their advice and technical expertise in the production of this publication. A particular word of appreciation is due to Richard Burke for his skill and unending patience in the design and layout of the final production.

The Central Remedial Clinic is a national organisation for the care, treatment and development of children and adults with a wide range of disabilities. Included in the services of the Central Remedial Clinic are training programmes in Desktop Publishing, Graphic Design, and In-plant Printing. This production is an outcome of that training.

Introduction

As a young boy growing up in the Liberties of Dublin I joined the Boy Scouts in Merchants Quay in 1950. Our main activities were hiking and camping in the Dublin/Wicklow Mountains. The geographic range of our outdoor pursuits was dictated to a large extent by our cycling abilities and the limited network of bus routes then available to us. One of our favourite expeditions was to Massy Woods, near Rockbrook. Even at that young age the woods had a magnetic attraction. We regularly lit our cooking fire in the old walled garden, within what I now know to be the foundation of a Richard Turner conservatory. Killakee House had long since been demolished, but a regular haunt of ours was the remains of the basement of the house, which held a fascination for us, and was the location for endless war games, which were then the rage.

During one of our expeditions into the basement we emerged to see an elderly gentlemen standing nearby. He smiled at us, gave a little wave, and walked off into the woods. Our scout leader later told us that the man we had seen was Lord Massy, that he once owned the woods and had lived in a beautiful mansion, which had stood over the basement we played in, but which had been taken from him because he owed money to the bank. He also told us that Lord Massy now lived in a little cottage nearby. I never saw Lord Massy again but I remembered the story, and I can still see him in my mind waving to us and walking slowly off into the woods.

Over the years I have visited Massy Woods many times and the beauty and tranquillity of the place constantly uplifts me. I often wondered about the story of Lord Massy and how he came to lose his beautiful house and demesne. I met people who, like myself, had snippets of the story, but I could not find anyone who had the whole story. I decided to find out for myself. It has been a fascinating journey that has taken me down many avenues and to places and people that I would never have otherwise encountered.

The story of the family of Lord Massy of Duntrileague is worth telling. It encapsulates the story of the Protestant Ascendancy in Ireland from its beginnings to its ultimate and inevitable collapse. In its later years the story of the family of Lord Massy is one of considerable emotional distress. I have tried to deal with the events of those years in a fair and sensitive manner. It is my hope that those reading the story will come to better understand the human side of the decline of the Protestant Ascendancy in Ireland, as seen through the history of the family of Lord Massy of Duntrileague.

Frank Tracy

THE MASSY STORY

Massy

Normandy

The Massy (de Massey) lineage can be traced to Normandy where they were landowners in the ninth century. Various locations in Normandy have been suggested for the origins of the branch of the family that subsequently accompanied William the Conqueror to England in 1066. It is most likely that this branch of the family originated in Massy in Avranches, rather than in Massy near Bayeux, as they seem to have been associates of Hugh of Avranches, known as Hugh Lupus, a nephew of William the Conqueror, who became Earl of Chester in 1071.

England

Harold Goodwin became King of England in 1066 following the death of his brother-in-law, Edward the Confessor, who died childless. William, Duke of Normandy, claimed that Edward, his great uncle, had promised him the English throne. He enlisted the support of knights from Normandy to invade England. Amongst William's supporters was his nephew, Hugh Lupus of Avranches. Harold, meanwhile, prepared to defend his throne. He firstly had to deal with his brother Hardrada, King of Norway, who also laid claim to the English throne. In September 1066 Hardrada invaded Yorkshire but was defeated by Harold's armies. Some days later, on the night of September 27th 1066, William set sail from Normandy with a fleet of 1,000 boats. Because Harold was in Yorkshire dealing with Hardrada's invasion, William's landing in Sussex met with no opposition. William waited for Harold's exhausted army to arrive from Yorkshire. The two armies engaged in battle at Sandlake near Hastings on the southern English coast on October 14, 1066. Harold was killed and his army defeated.

> *The carnage was great. It is said that in the English ranks the only*
> *movement was the dropping of the dead, the living stood motionless ever*
> *ready with their steel, those sons of the old Saxon race, the most dauntless*
> *of men. As darkness fell the ring of steel dwindled until all Wessex Thanes*
> *and soldiers lay dead around their King.*

(Makers of the Realm. Arthur Bryant. Collins, London 1953.)

On Christmas Day 1066, William was crowned King of England at
Westminster. He followed up his victory with widespread confiscation of
Saxon lands and at the time of his death in 1087 almost all of the estates
in England were in Norman ownership. William was accompanied to
England by many Norman knights who were rewarded with grants of
land confiscated from their Saxon owners. Among these Norman knights
were the de Masseys. The Falaise Roll is a record of the names of the
companions of Duke William. The following is an extract from the Roll.

> *HUGUE DE MACEY. From Macey, near Pontorson and Mon-St-Michel,*
> *arrondissemont Avranches, Normandy...... Hugo de Maci held in*
> *Huntingsdonshire in 1086, and Hamo de Macy possessed nine lordships*
> *in Cheshire from Hugh Lupus, having been one of the palatinate barons*
> *who built his castle at Dunham Massey. In 1093, Hamo de Macey*
> *subscribed to the foundation charter of Chester Abbey to which he granted*
> *lands....Hamon and Roland de Macey are mentioned in several*
> *declarations of fiefs of Mon-St-Michel in 1172. The family remained*
> *prominent in England and from them sprung the barons Massey.*

(Falaise Roll. M.Jackson & Leonce Macary. London 1938.
Reprinted 1994 by the Genealogical Publishing Company Baltimore.)

Following the victory of Duke William, Sir Hamon de Massey, who had
command of a division of archers at Hastings under Hugh Lupus, was
granted considerable possessions in 1070 by Hugh Lupus, then Earl of
Chester. One of these possessions was an estate at Dunham, which had
been confiscated from a Saxon landowner called Alweard. At the same
time Sir Hamon was created a baron. A long line of de Masseys
subsequently resided on the Dunham estate, all with the Christian name

Hamon. The town of Altrincham received its charter from Hamon VI in 1290 and a celebration was held there in 1990 to commemorate the 700th anniversary of the event. The family provided many High Sheriffs and Chief Justices, and also filled many other administrative posts in Cheshire over the years. In the years subsequent to the Norman invasion the Masseys spread to many parts of Cheshire and adjoining counties. There were about sixteen families of Masseys in Cheshire by the seventeenth century. They settled in Coddington, Puddington, Sale, Broxton, Graston, Alresford, Tatton, Wincham, Timperley, Edgerley, Kensall and Dunfield. According to the Cheshire Heraldry Centre, one branch of the Cheshire Masseys emigrated to Salem, Massachusetts about 1630. In that line was Hart Almerin Massey, the founder of the Massey-Ferguson firm. His grandson Charles Vincent, born in 1887, became the first Canadian to serve as Governor-General of Canada, and his younger brother Raymond achieved fame as a stage and film actor.

After the death of Hamon VI without a male heir in 1341 there occurred a long dispute over the Dunham Massey property. There are many versions of the dispute, which involved the Masseys of Tatton and others. Cecily, who was the daughter (or sister, according to Collins Peerage) of Hamon VI married a John Fitton in 1295 and the property eventually descended in the Fitton female line to the Booths of Cheshire. In 1736 the property was passed down, again in the female line, from the Booths to the Greys, Earls of Stamford, who held it until it was handed over to the National Trust in 1976. To-day, Dunham-Massey is one of the major heritage visitor attractions in Cheshire.

The French lands of the family reverted to the crown of France when the male line died out. A Tower of London record (Rot. Norman, 6, Hen, 5. 1419) states:

> *The King granted unto James Hugonet the lands and territories which the Lord of Massy held in the vice-county of Bayeux: whence it seems that the ancient hereditary Estates of these Lords in Normandy, reverted to the crown upon the decease of the last Baron of Dunham-Massey*

Captain Hugh Massy (Hugh I)

In 1641 Catholic landowners in Ireland rebelled against strictures imposed on them by the English Crown. Bitter fighting ensued and many atrocities were committed, particularly against the Protestant population. Hugh Massy was a cavalry officer with a force sent by King Charles I to crush the rebellion in Ireland. Although he was almost certainly one of the Cheshire Masseys, exhaustive work by many researchers has failed to definitively link him with any particular branch of that family. The clues to his family origin are conflicting. Hugh I adopted the coat of arms of the Sale Masseys, but there is no record of him in their genealogy. The only Massey family of that period to make consistent use of the name Hugh was that of Edgerley, who were descended from the Masseys of Coddington.

Hugh I was a captain of cavalry when he first came to Ireland. He returned to England after the 1641 expedition and, following the outbreak of civil war in England in 1642, joined the forces of the Parliamentarians against Charles I. In 1644 Arundel Castle was captured by Parliamentary forces and Hugh I was appointed Constable of Arundel. In 1647 he was back in Ireland as part of an army commanded by Colonel Michael Jones that left Dublin on August 8th to relieve the town of Trim, which was being besieged by Catholic Confederates under Thomas Preston. Following the execution of Charles I on January 30th 1649, Oliver Cromwell was appointed Lord Lieutenant of Ireland, and on August 15th 1649 landed at the mouth of the River Liffey near Dublin with a large and well-equipped army of 8,000 infantry, 3,000 light cavalry and 1,200 dragoons to suppress the Irish rebellion. Hugh I served with the Cromwellian forces as a captain in the First Troop of Horse, in a regiment commanded by Col. Chidley-Coote, and campaigned mainly in Limerick and Tipperary.

The Irish rebel forces were led by the royalist Earl of Ormonde and Lord Inchiquin, Protestant landowners based in Leinster and Munster respectively. In the North, the Catholic Owen Roe O'Neill, nephew of Hugh O'Neill the exiled Earl of Tyrone, returned from the Spanish

Netherlands to lead the rebel forces in Ulster. O'Neill hoped to take advantage of the rebellion to regain his family's landholdings in Ulster. Ormonde and Inchiquin were largely ineffective military leaders, losing a succession of major encounters against Parliamentary forces. O'Neill however was a brilliant military strategist, a fact openly acknowledged by Cromwell, who treated O'Neill's forces with great caution.

The sudden death of Owen Roe O'Neill in November 1649 removed the Confederation's most effective military leader. Over the following two years Cromwell's armies ruthlessly suppressed supporters of the Confederation. Ormonde, Inchiquin and Owen Roe's nephew Daniel fled Ireland in December 1650. Ormonde and Inchiquin had their lands returned 12 years later upon the restoration of the English monarchy. The O'Neills did not have their lands returned. By the end of 1652 the rebellion was effectively crushed. Over 40,000 Irish rebel soldiers and their families were transported as slaves to sugar plantations in the West Indies and tobacco plantations in Virginia. Few ever returned. In 1653 a total of 20 million acres of land was confiscated and apportioned out among new Protestant owners in repayment for services rendered during the military campaign.

Under an Act of the English Parliament the value of land for sale to military campaigners in Ireland was set at £200 per thousand acres in Ulster, £300 in Connaught, £450 in Munster and £600 in Leinster. Acreage was determined by the Irish measure of 7,231 sq. yards as against the English measure of 4,840 sq. yards. The cost of land acquisition was offset against wage arrears, which stood at £1,550,000 at the end of the campaign. A further Act of Parliament enabled purchasers to double their land allocation for an extra quarter of the price. The Cromwellian land settlements established the Protestant Ascendancy as the predominant ruling class in Ireland for the next 250 years.

In 1659, following the successful outcome of the Cromwellian campaign in Ireland, Captain Hugh Massy (Hugh I) acquired landholdings totalling around 1,800 Irish acres at three locations near Galbally in Co. Limerick in lieu of military wage arrears. These landholdings previously belonged to John Cantwell, Henry Wall and John Burgett, Catholic landowners and descendants of Norman settlers who had been granted their lands by the Crown in the 13th century. Part of the landholdings acquired from John Cantwell comprised 263 acres at Duntrileague, Co. Limerick. The name Duntrileague comes from the Gaelic Dún Trí Liag , the Fort of Three Pillar Stones, a nearby megalithic tomb. Captain Massy established his demesne at Duntrileague, where he built a residence. He married Margaret Percy, by whom he had a son, Hugh, and a daughter, Elizabeth. He married a second wife, by whom he had a second son Samuel, and two daughters, Alice and Mary. He subsequently married a third, fourth and fifth time, but had no further children. Hugh I probably died about 1691. Earlier that year he had transferred ownership of Duntrileague to his eldest son, Hugh II. An early family history, *Pedigree of Lord Massy*, states that the Deed of Settlement for the transfer from father to son was drawn up in a Limerick inn and that *"Hugh, the elder, knew that his time was but short."*

Hugh Massy (Hugh II)

Hugh Massy, eldest son of Captain Hugh Massy (Hugh I) and Margaret Percy, was probably born in England prior to the acquisition of Duntrileague in 1659 and arrived in Ireland after that date. A book, *Footprints of a Faithful Servant*, written by the Rev. Dawson Massy records the following of Hugh II's time at Duntrileague:- *"During the next thirty years he remained there undisturbed, and trebled his possessions by divine blessing on his industry."*

© *Massy (Stoneville) Collection*

Hugh II married Amy Benson of the North of Ireland, and had four sons, Hugh, John (ancestor of the Ingoldsby Massys), William (ancestor of the

Stoneville Massys), and Charles (ancestor of the Dillon Massys), and two daughters, Margaret and Amy. At its most prosperous the Duntrileague property extended to 2,293 acres. In 1674 Hugh II was appointed High Sheriff for Co. Limerick. He also built the church at Duntrileague, the ruined tower of which still stands. His father Hugh I made a present of a bell to the church.

Duntrileague Church, Co. Limerick
© *the authors collection*

The period from the accession of the Catholic King James II in 1685, to the battle of the Boyne in 1690, brought terror to the Protestant population in Ireland who believed that they would see a repeat of the atrocities of 1641. An Act of Attainder listed nearly 2,500 Protestants who were condemned to death. Hugh I and Hugh II were listed, as was Anthony Irby, who was rector of Duntrileague. His wife Elizabeth, Hugh I's daughter, was out of the country during this troubled time. When she returned, she was overjoyed at finding her husband, father and brother still alive. In thanksgiving she gave a beautiful silver chalice, exquisitely inscribed, to Duntrileague Church:

> *This Chalice was given by Elizabeth Irby to ye Church of Duntryleage in the Kingdome of Ireland as a grateful acknowledgement to Almighty God for her safe Returne to her native Country and findeing her Husband and Father in good health: which Mercy she hopes never to forget.*

The Chalice is of London silver, probably made between 1678 and 1690 and is in the safekeeping of the Dean of Cashel.

After King James II's flight to France, following his defeat at the Battle of the Boyne, fighting continued around Limerick. At Christmas 1690, Hugh II visited the Cromwellian General Ginkel at Bansha about 20 miles east of Duntrileague and he obtained a troop of forty dragoons to protect his house. On his return he found the house at Duntrileague in flames. He managed to save an outbuilding in which he lived until a replacement house was built. Hugh II died at Duntrileague in 1701 and is reputed to be buried under the floor of the church.

Colonel Hugh Massy (Hugh III)

Hugh Massy, eldest son of Hugh Massy (Hugh II) and Amy Benson, was born in 1685*. He married Elizabeth Evans of Caharas, Co. Limerick, and had seven sons, Hugh, George, John, Godfrey (ancestor of Massys of Kingswell, and Massys of Grantstown Hall), William (ancestor of Canadian Massys), Eyre and Charles, and four daughters, Mary, Amy, Elizabeth (ancestor of Massy-Westropps) and Catherine. He was High Sheriff for County Limerick in 1711 and by 1722 he was a colonel commanding a troop of horse militia, *"being a strenuous advocate of the Reformation….. and keeping a watchful eye over*

© *Massy (Stoneville) Collection*

the Papists who were then disposed to be very troublesome to the peace and good government of the realm." Hugh III lived through the height of the Penal Laws in Ireland. He died on 19th November 1757 *"after a tedious illness"* and is quite probably buried at Duntrileague. The Massy family at this time had landholdings and residences throughout east Limerick, the nearby Glen of Aherlow in Co. Tipperary, and in Co. Cork. They gained a reputation for constant entertaining, gambling and duelling. During his lifetime Hugh III had mortgaged all of the family holdings in Duntrileague and in Co. Cork. These debts were eventually settled by the second Baron Massy who married an heiress.

---

* There is some doubt about the accuracy of this date, as this would
  mean he fathered his eldest son at the early age of fifteen.

Hugh Fitzjohn Massy

In 1743 a dramatic event occurred which had a profound effect on relations between two prominent Cromwellian families in Co. Limerick, the Massys and the Ingoldsbys. Both families were descended from Cromwellian campaigners. Henry and George Ingoldsby were officers who campaigned alongside Captain Hugh Massy under Cromwell. Both families were granted estates in Co. Limerick as part of the Cromwellian plantation. Like the Massys, the Ingoldsbys subsequently amassed extensive landholdings and held positions of prominence in Co. Limerick.

Hugh Fitzjohn Massy was a son of John Massy who was a brother of Hugh III. Frances Ingoldsby was a daughter, and co-heiress with her sister Catherine, of Henry Ingoldsby M.P. who died in 1731. It is said that Frances inherited an annual income of £900 a year. It is also said that Frances was secretly married in 1741 by a Catholic priest to Jack Williams, a servant in the family who was alleged to have been an illegitimate son of her father, Henry Ingoldsby. Subsequent attempts by Jack Williams to prove his marriage to Frances Ingoldsby were not successful.

On the night of 13th November 1743, Hugh Fitzjohn Massy, his brother-in-law John Bourcher and some others gained entry to Nantenen rectory near Rathkeale, Co. Limerick where Frances Ingoldsby was residing under the guardianship of Reverend Thomas Royse, whose wife was a relative of Frances. Under threat of violence they kidnapped Frances Ingoldsby and made off with her to the safety of Massy lands in the Galtee Mountains. A reward of £200 was placed on Massy and Bourcher's heads by the government. Massy, accompanied by Frances, made his escape to Bordeaux in France. At some stage a marriage ceremony took place and Frances seems to have succumbed to the situation. It is clear that the objective of the abduction was to secure an income for Hugh Massy.

In summer 1744 the couple returned to Ireland. Massy and Bourcher were charged with abduction and bailed to appear in court. The first case was heard in Cork in 1745. The Massy family, and particularly Hugh Fitzjohn's uncle Dean Charles Massy, exerted their considerable influence on the grand jury and the charge was dismissed. A subsequent case in Limerick had the same outcome. Massy and Bourcher were released and the reality of the marriage was accepted. The outcome of the case probably suited Frances Ingoldsby as the female victims of abduction were often regarded subsequently as soiled and unlikely to attract the attention of appropriate suitors. Hugh Fitzjohn and Frances Massy had two children, a daughter born in 1744 after her return to Ireland and a son, Hugh Ingoldsby Massy, born in 1749. Edward Spencer, a contemporary, wrote in 1746 that Hugh Fitzjohn Massy *'has the misfortune of not being liked or regarded by any person of figure or character in this county.'* Frances Ingoldsby Massy died at Clonarold, near Stoneville, Co. Limerick in 1755. (A full account of the abduction of Frances Ingoldsby is the subject of an excellent book, The Abduction of a Limerick Heiress by Toby Barnard. Irish Academic Press).

Hugh, 1st Baron Massy of Duntrileague

Hugh Massy, eldest son of Colonel Hugh Massy (Hugh III) and Elizabeth Evans, was born in 1700. He succeeded his father as Colonel of his Regiment of Horse Militia and was appointed Sheriff of Co. Limerick in 1739. He was M.P. for Co. Limerick 1759-76 and for Old Leighlin 1776. On 4th August 1776 he was created Lord Massy, 1st Baron of Duntrileague, taking his seat in Parliament on 18th December 1777. He married Mary Dawson of Newforest, Co. Tipperary in 1733 and had three sons, Hugh, James (ancestor of Massy-Dawsons) and John, and one daughter Elizabeth.

© *Guinness Family Collection*

He subsequently married Rebecca Delap from Antigua on 16th March 1754 by whom he had another three sons and three daughters. He had residences at Duntrileague, Stagdale Lodge, Suir Castle and Paradise (Massy) Lodge, which was built in 1776. He died on 30th January 1788, aged 88, at Stagdale Lodge, Co. Tipperary.

The Freeman's Journal of 7th February 1788 contains the following death notice:-

> *At his seat at Stagdale Lodge, the Right Honourable Hugh, Lord Baron Massy. He is succeeded in his title and extensive fortune by the Hon. Hugh Massy, Member of Parliament for the county of Limerick.*

Eyre Massey, 1st Baron Clarina of Elm Park

Eyre Massey, sixth son of Colonel Hugh Massy (Hugh III) and younger brother of the 1st Baron Massy of Duntrileague, was born on 24th May, 1719. He had a very distinguished military career. Having purchased a commission in the 27th Foot (the Enniskillings) he was promoted to Lieutenant in the Grenadiers and saw action in the War of Austrian Succession (1740-48) and in the Seven Years War (1756-63). In 1739 he was with the expeditionary forces that captured Portobello in Panama. Returning to England he was wounded at the battle of Culloden. He was promoted to Captain in 1751 and Major in 1755 and in 1759 he was with the British Army under General Wolfe that invaded Canada and captured Quebec. Eyre returned to Ireland in 1769 and was promoted to Major General in 1776. For the next four years he commanded the British troops at Halifax, Nova Scotia. He returned, finally, to

© *Massy (Stoneville) Collection*

Ireland in 1794 and was made a full General in 1796 at the age of 77. After a period as Governor of Limerick and Governor of the Royal Hospital at Kilmainham in Dublin, he was created Marshall of the Army in Ireland, which position he held until his death in 1804. Eyre Massey sat in the Irish Parliament from 1790 to 1797 and was created a Baron in December 1800, as Lord Clarina of Elm Park. The Clarina title was what is known as a Union Peerage in that it was granted in return for support for the Act of Union in the Irish House of Commons. A particular feature of the Clarinas is that they re-inserted an 'e' into their surname (i.e. Massey), to distinguish their lineage from the Massys of Duntrileague. In 1804, at the age of 85, Eyre Massey set off to take the waters at Bath and died there on May 17th. His wife Catherine died in 1815 and they are both buried in Bath Abbey. Eyre's grandson, also named Eyre, the third Lord Clarina, married Susan Barton. Susan's great-nephew was Erskine Childers (1870-1922) who was executed during the Irish Civil War. Childer's son, also Erskine, was President of Ireland in 1973/74. The Clarina title became extinct in 1952 with the death of Eyre Nathaniel Massey, 6th Baron Clarina, who died without male issue.

Archdeacon George Massy

The first Baron Massy of Duntrileague had another brother, the Rev. George Massy, Archdeacon of Ardfert, of whom an amusing story has been passed down. In 1750 he made a journey from Limerick to Dublin in pursuit of a more favourable posting which had recently become vacant. At that time it took four days coach travel to make the journey. In the course of conversation with his fellow passengers during the journey the Rev. Massy ascertained that one of them was also a clergyman travelling to Dublin seeking the same post. On arrival in Dublin, George Massy made straight for Dublin Castle and succeeded in getting the

© *Massy (Stoneville) Collection*

relevant official to interview him there and then. He impressed the official, who granted him the post. On his way out of the Castle he passed the other applicant, who had gone to his hotel to wash and change into his best clothes, arriving for his interview. On meeting him the official said, "*How unlucky you are, sir. Dirty Boots, whom you must have met on his way out, has just got the post.*" Archdeacon Massy revelled in retelling the story, and became known for the rest of his life as, Dirty Boots. When he died at the ripe old age of eighty in 1782 he left his estate to his younger brother, Eyre, the 1st Baron Clarina.

Hugh, 2nd Baron Massy of Duntrileague

Hugh Massy, eldest son of the 1st Baron and Mary Dawson was born on 14th April 1733. Appointed Sheriff of Co. Limerick in 1763; he was M.P. for Askeaton 1776-83 and Co. Limerick 1783-88. On Sept 25 1760, he married Catherine Taylor of Askeaton, Co. Limerick and had four sons, Hugh, Edward, George-Eyre (ancestor of Riversdale Massys) and John (ancestor of Massy-Beresfords), and four daughters Mary-Anne, Catherine, Jane and Sarah. His wife, Catherine, was the elder daughter and co-heiress with her half sister, Sarah Countess of Carrick, of Col. Edward Taylor of Ballynort, Co. Limerick. Catherine inherited considerable property near Askeaton. Her mother Anne had also been an heiress. Catherine brought some £5,000 in cash plus "half the Barony of Askeaton" to the marriage. Her fortune was later used by the 2nd Baron to settle Massy family debts still outstanding from Hugh III. The second baron succeeded to the title in January 1788, and died just 2 years later on 10th May 1790, aged 57, at William Street Dublin. His wife Catherine died in August 1791. According to Thom's Directory he had residences at Duntrileague, Paradise (Massy) Lodge, Stagdale Lodge, Suir Castle and Ballynort.

Hugh, 3rd Baron Massy of Duntrileague

Hugh Massy, eldest son of the 2nd Baron and Catherine Taylor was born on 24th October 1761.He married Margaret Everina Barton of the Grove, Co. Tipperary on 12th March 1792 at Port Patrick, and had four sons,

Hugh Hamon, George William, John and Dawson, and five daughters Grace Elizabeth, Cathenne, Susan Maria, Margaret Everina and Elizabeth Jane. He succeeded to the title in May 1790. In 1800 Lord Massy was one of only 26 Representative Irish Peers, out of a total of 101, who voted against the Act of Union in the Irish House of Lords. Two branches of the Massy family, therefore, took opposing sides on the Act of Union.

Around 1790 the 3rd Baron moved the seat of Lord Massy from Duntrileague, initially to Massy Lodge near Anglesboro, Co.

© Massy (Stoneville) Collection

Limerick and later in 1807 to Hermitage in Castleconnell, Co. Limerick. Hermitage was an imposing mansion of 37 rooms and 24 outhouses on the banks of the river Shannon. Built in 1800 for a banker named Bruce, it was subsequently purchased by Lord Massy.

Hermitage, Castleconnell, Co Limerick
© Guinness Family Collection

It was during the closing years of the 3rd Baron's life that a mausoleum or 'Charnel House' was built beside Duntrileague Church. The first interment in the Charnel House was Elizabeth Massy, wife of the Baron's brother George Eyre, who died on 25th February 1811. The Charnel House at Duntrileague contains 26 Massy coffins, stacked to the roof and covering a period of

The Charnel House, Duntrileague
© The Authors Collection

time from 1811 to 1931. Hugh Massy, 3rd Baron of Duntrileague, died on 20th June 1812, aged 50, at Hermitage, and was interred in the Charnel House at Duntrileague. His residences are listed as Hermitage, Stagdale Lodge, Massy Lodge, and Suir Castle.

The Limerick Evening Post of Wednesday June 24th, 1812, contained the following death notice:-

> *On Sunday morning inst. at three o'clock the Right Honourable Hugh Massy, Lord Baron Massy, died at his seat, Hermitage, in this county, to the inexplicable grief of his truly affectionate and disconsolate family – and regret of his numerous tenantry and friends. He is succeeded in his title and estates by his son Hugh, a minor, now Lord Baron Massy.*

Rev. Charles Massy

The 3rd Baron had a relative in the Dillon-Massy branch of the family, Rev. Charles Massy, who was involved in one of the most celebrated court cases of the day. Rev. Massy was married to a young lady who was renowned for her beauty and high spirits. He had church connections with Co. Meath and was a good friend of Lord Headford who was a frequent visitor to the Rev. Massy's household. Lord Headford and Mrs Massy formed a romantic relationship even though she was a young woman and he was a grey haired elderly gentleman. One Sunday while the Rev. Massy was conducting religious services in his local church, his wife ran away with Lord Headford. The couple travelled by boat from Doonass on the Clare side of the River Shannon to an awaiting carriage on the Limerick side.

Rev. Massy took a case against Lord Headford for "criminal conversation" with his wife. It was the first such case ever brought in Ireland and was regarded as sensational at the time. The case was heard in Ennis Court on 27 July 1804 and a transcript of it can be read in the National Library of Ireland. In presenting the case to court on behalf of Rev. Massy, his counsel Mr Bartholomew Hoare referred to Lord Headford as" *this hoary veteran in whom, like Etna, the snow above did not quench the flames below*". After a lengthy hearing, the Jury found in Rev.

Massy's favour and he was awarded £10,000, a very considerable sum of money at that time. Lord Headford had no trouble paying the award, as his yearly income from his estates was £40,000 per annum.

Hugh Hamon, 4th Baron Massy of Duntrileague

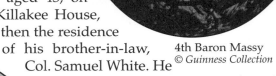

Hugh Hamon Massy, son of the 3rd Baron and Margaret Everina Barton, was born on 13th February 1793. He married Matilda White, youngest daughter of Luke White of Woodlands, Co. Dublin, on 22nd June 1826 and had two sons, Hugh Hamon, and John Thomas. He succeeded to the title in June 1812, aged 19 years, and died, aged 43, on 27th September 1836, at Killakee House, Rathfarnham, Co. Dublin, then the residence of his brother-in-law, Col. Samuel White. He

4th Baron Massy
© *Guinness Collection*

is buried in Castleconnell. Although he died at a young age, the 4th Baron's marriage to Luke White's daughter, Matilda, was to have very significant consequences for the family's future.

The following obituary appeared in the Freeman's Journal of Monday October 3rd 1836:-

Baroness Matilda Massy
© *Guinness Collection*

DEATH OF LORD MASSY

We are concerned to announce the most painful intelligence of the death of this highly esteemed and honoured nobleman, which sad event took place on Tuesday last, the 27th instant, by fever at Killakee, where his lordship had been residing for the last few weeks, on account of his lordship's delicate state of health. This deplored event has thrown the relatives and numerous connexions of Lord Massy into the deepest affliction; and the regret, as far as the news has already spread, is universal. In Limerick, the sympathy of all classes in the sorrow of the afflicted family evinces the respect and estimation in which his lordship was held. His lordship has left two sons, who are both at a tender age. The Rt. Hon. Hugh Hamon, Lord Massy, was born 13th February 1793. He succeeded to the dignity of fourth baron of that title on the demise of his noble father in June 1812. He married, June 1826, Matilda, youngest daughter of the late Luke White Esq. of Dublin. Lady Massy was left on Tuesday in the most poignant grief at the loss of her beloved partner.

Luke White

Luke White, Matilda White's father, was born in 1752 and became one of the richest and most successful businessmen of the late-eighteenth century. Not a great deal is known of his origins and background. Popular stories have been told about his humble beginnings as a book auctioneer's apprentice, or of his finding a lottery ticket in a book from which he won £20,000. There is, however, no historical evidence supporting any of these stories. The evidence that does exist suggests that he came from a financially comfortable family in Cork. His brother, Thomas White, was an established

© *Guinness Collection*

bookseller in Cork. There is also some evidence that his family may have been second or third generation Huguenots. It is known that in the early years of the eighteenth century some Huguenot families named Leblanc settled in Ireland, and it is possible that the name White is an English adaptation of that name. A further indication of possible Huguenot origins is the fact that his first wife, Elizabeth de la Maziére, whom he married in February 1781, was definitely of Huguenot descent. It was probably with the support of his family that Luke White established a bookselling business in Dublin in 1775. He combined his bookselling business with the acquisition of various properties in the city. In 1777 he ventured into the risky business of becoming a lottery agent, at which he was extremely successful. In 1789 he sold his retail bookselling business, and concentrated on wholesale bookselling, financial investments, and the lottery. It is believed that by 1799 he was worth over £500,000, making him one of the richest businessmen in Ireland.

In 1800 he purchased an estate at Luttrellstown, including Luttrellstown Castle, for £96,000 from the 2nd Earl of Carhampton. He paid Lord Carhampton a deposit of £40,000 to secure the deal. Lord Carhampton, however, quickly regretted his decision to sell Luttrellstown and he wrote to White *"on consultation with my family, I wish to withdraw from the sale."* He offered to return the £40,000 deposit to White plus an additional payment of £40,000 in compensation. White's reply was characteristic of the man. *"Luke White"* he wrote *"never yet consulted with his family or made a bargain which he regretted."* The sale of Luttrellstown to Luke White was

concluded. Around the same time, White purchased land at Killakee (Coill á Chaeich - Blind Man's Wood) in the foothills of the Dublin Mountains, which was previously owned by the Conolly family of Castletown, Co. Kildare, and he built a truly beautiful house there.

Killakee House, Co Dublin
© *Guinness family collection*

Killakee House was a 36-roomed two-storeyed stucco-faced house of symmetrical aspect with a curved bow in the centre front and similar bows in the gables. It had a balustraded parapet to the roof, a veranda with slender iron uprights and a balcony above along the centre of the front, which gave the house the appearance of a Mediterranean villa.

Interior of Killakee House
© *Guinness family collection*

The Killakee estate also contained the infamous Hellfire Club on the summit of Mount Pelier. At the time Luke White acquired the estate, the Hellfire Club was already in a ruinous state.

In 1803 LukeWhite bought the Lareen Estate at Kinlough, Co. Leitrim,

Interior of Killakee House
© *Guinness family collection*

close to the Leitrim/Donegal border, from William and Elizabeth Thompson. In 1807 he bought more land in Leitrim from Sir George Hill and John Beresford. He also bought land in Co. Longford. Luke White's principle residence was Luttrellstown Castle, and Lareen was his sporting estate. He was elected High Sheriff for Leitrim in 1807 and was elected a Member of Parliament from 1818 until his death in 1824. He was married twice, having ten children, five sons and four daughters by his first wife Eliza Maziére, and one son by his second wife Arabella Fortescue. He was also an active governor of many charitable foundations. The Countess of Hardwick, wife of the then Lord Lieutenant of Ireland, said of Luke White in 1803 *"Good luck accompanied him in every speculation, and he knew how to profit by it, but with the fairest fame."* Luke White died in London on 25 February 1824 and he is buried in the Church of Ireland graveyard at Clonsilla Co. Dublin. In his will he divided his properties in South County Dublin between his eldest sons, Col Thomas White and Colonel Samuel White, and property at Rathcline, Co. Longford was left to his third son, Luke Jnr. The Leitrim estates were divided between Col. Samuel White and Luke Jnr, Samuel getting the Duncarbery and Aghavoghil estates, and Luke Jnr. getting Lareen, Mullinaleck and Rosfriar.

Luke White's fourth son, Henry, inherited the Luttrellstown estate and was created Lord Annaly in 1863. Luttrellstown Castle was the seat of Lord Anally for many years. The Hon. Ernest Guinness bought it in 1927 as a wedding present for his daughter. With her marriage the estate passed into the ownership of the Plunkett family. It was sold again in the 1980s and is now a luxury hotel. The final connection of the Whites with Ireland ended with the sale of Gowran Castle, Co. Kilkenny. Gowran Castle was the seat of Viscount Clifden. It was inherited by the daughter of the 3rd Viscount Clifden who married the 3rd Lord Annaly. The 4th Lord Annaly sold Gowran Castle in 1955. The Annaly title remains in the White family, who now live in England.

Tradition has it that the Whites were good landlords, and their tenants were able to negotiate reasonable rents. There are also many records of schools, churches and other public works financed by the Whites. Luke White is said to have contributed to the acceleration of the emancipation of Catholics in Ireland by the spirited manner in which he expended £200,000 in contesting elections with the opponents of that measure.

Another example of Luke White's public beneficence was uncovered in a most unexpected location. On 2 October 2001 a copper alloy dedication plaque was discovered in the foundation of Nelson's Pillar on Dublin's O' Connell Street, which had been blown up in 1966. The site was being excavated in preparation for the erection of the new Dublin Spire to replace Nelson's Pillar. The plaque was found under a Portland stone slab and was inscribed with a dedication to Lord Nelson and a list of Dublin merchants and bankers who contributed to the cost of the monument. Included in the list of subscribers is Luke White.

Colonel Samuel White

Samuel White, second son of Luke White, was an officer of the Dublin County Militia. He was High Sheriff for Leitrim in 1809 and replaced his father in the House of Commons from 1825–1847. He also held lands in his own right at Woodtown some two kilometres down the road from Killakee. A map from the early 1800s shows Samuel White living in considerable style on an estate of some 2,900 acres at Killakee, half of which was let out to tenants. Samuel White laid out the gardens at Killakee in exquisite splendour. Terraced lawns were laid out with shrubs and trees. A large water fountain graced the front lawn, the remains of which can still be seen today. A particular feature at Killakee was an avenue lined with Chilean Pine (monkey-puzzle) trees. A walled garden in a secluded vale in the nearby woods contained further fountains and magnificent curvilinear conservatories by Richard Turner, which contained many exotic plants.

© *Guinness family collection*

An article in the Gardeners' Chronicle and Agricultural Gazette of Dec. 10th 1864 by William Robinson gives a very detailed description of the Killakee gardens in their prime, of which the following are some extracts:-

The visitor to Dublin, fond of gardening, and fond too of beautiful scenery, cannot enjoy so satisfying a combination of both in any place of which I am

acquainted, as at Killakee, situated about 7 miles from Dublin, on Montpelier, a ruin-crested hill, which may be distinctly seen from most parts of the Bay of Dublin. The house is built near the top of the hill on its east side, is surrounded by a fine and chaste terrace garden, and literally looks down on Dublin and its environs for miles around....... The day of my visit was fortunately a pretty clear one...... To the north could be seen the mountains of Mourne......to the east, between the Park and the sea, lay the fair city of Dublin itself. To the south the view was interrupted by the high hills of Killakee and others, forming an amphitheatre around that side of Dublin; but there were charming views of the hills of Killiney and Dalkey, with as good a bird's eye view of the Kingstown harbour as of Dublin.

Though the mountains around are bleak, rocky and barren, Killakee has its woods and pines, its rhododendrons and rare shrubs, as well as the richest lowlands, all planted by the late Colonel Samuel White...... The entrance front of the house is to the west; the eastern one, looking towards Dublin, and perfectly commanding the view I have already alluded to, opens to the terrace garden; while on the north side of the house is a garden of American plants, and on the south a Rose Garden of like dimensions. An exquisitely furnished saloon occupies the greater part of the front of the house, and from every window of this the lovely scene may be enjoyed from a fresh point of view. The central windows open, and by a wide flight of steps a walk nearly 400 feet long and 20 wide is reached. At the base of this terrace, and high slope of velvety grass, are 18 circles of choice roses; and at some distance from, but immediately in front of the great central flight of steps leading from the terrace to the lower level, is a fine circular fountain, with a bronze Neptune in his car of shells drawn by sea horses, a pair of very symmetrical specimens of Araucaria Imbricata about 24 feet high, standing on each side on the lawn to the right and left of the fountain.

The drive, about a mile in length from the chief entrance lodge, passes down through the woods between the house and the abruptly rising hill, which to many persons, would present as great an attraction as the gardens by which the house is flanked....... to the south of the lawn is a picturesque and densely wooded glen, with mountain rivulet running for several miles through the demesne; and in this glen the principal gardens

Killakee Gardens

© *Guinness family collection*

are situated..... This garden, or the greater part of it, has been cut in the hill side, and from its wooded banks beyond the upper or southern end the visitor may look as plainly down upon the garden and its charms......The scene was most enchanting; for many feet below were mapped out the beauties of this unique garden, most conspicuous being one of Mr. Turner's best efforts – a very ornamental circular conservatory with a wing of curvilinear houses on each side, the end houses being circular, and the whole range – which stretches across the further and lower level of the garden – being of almost faultless symmetry and elegance.

The chief entrance to the garden is at the side of the upper level...in the centre of each half of the top level was a statue surrounded by a chain of 10 beds, well filled and well varied with plenty of verdure, and on it large cones of pillar roses...... the middle level was for the most part decorated with bedding plants, 30 neat beds of these surrounding a statue places in the centre of each half, with handsome Arancarias and very symmetrical Irish Yews.....The lower level had a handsome fountain and basin on each half, with a single chain of 10 beds encircling them....From the seat on the hill, whence this garden is so well seen, with the embowering woods around.......the visitor may by looking to the right, see one half of Dublin Bay, and apparently sleeping in it, the Hill of Howth .... The Bay of Dublin, and this beautiful geometrical garden, from one rustic chair!

Outside the lower end of the terrace garden...a remarkable structure was being erected.... it is a very singular and interesting Fernery, 60 feet long and about 20 feet wide, and 15 feet high. I know of no better example of the advantage of extensively planting and draining a barren and elevated district than is afforded by this demesne of 500 acres. The late Colonel White found it a barren waste, supporting here and there a few miserable cottiers; but before his death abundant wood had sheltered and beautified the scene; productive land began to yield ample return for outlay; garden beauty appeared upon hill and in ravine; and the geometrical garden spoken of, replaced an impassable thicket of briars. The gardens were laid out by Mr Niven, the well-known landscape gardener, and were made by Mr. W. Roylance, who, first as gardener and since as general superintendent, had charge of the place for nearly 20 years, during which time most of the gardens and garden improvements have been made......

these however are still continued by Mrs. White.....I have not yet seen the place in which the unities, so to speak, of good taste in laying out and keeping gardens, both geometrical and natural in style, are better preserved than at "Whites of Killakee."

Colonel Samuel White married Anne Salisbury Roth second daughter of George Roth of Salisbury Co. Kilkenny, but they had no children. He lived at Killakee House and divided his time between Dublin and London. He was only an occasional visitor to his Leitrim estates. He died on 27th May 1854 aged 70, and his wife Anne died aged 79, on 27th November 1880. They are both buried in Whitechurch Parish churchyard close to Killakee. The church contains some fine memorials to them.

Luke White (Jnr.)

Luke White Jnr. was MP for Longford for a time and High Sheriff of that county in 1821. Having inherited Lareen, Mullinaleck and Rossfriar from his father, he built Lareen House and spent most of his time there. He was unmarried. The 1835 Ordnance Survey name book notes that, in Lareen *"the appearance of the houses, gardens &c. speaks in favour of the industry of the inhabitants."* Luke White Jnr. died in the same year (1854) as his brother Samuel and is the only member of the White family to be buried in Leitrim. The inscription on his tombstone in Kinlough old cemetery reads *"To the memory of Luke White Esq. of Lareen in this county who departed this life on 19th August 1854 in the 69th year of his reign. Deeply regretted by his numerous friends."*

Samuel White made a will in 1853 leaving Duncarbery and Aghavoghil to his nephew, John Thomas William Massy. A month before his death, Luke White Jnr. also made a will leaving Lareen, Mullinaleck and Rossfriar to John Thomas Massy. With the death of the two White brothers the entire Leitrim estates passed to their nephew John Thomas Massy who, in time, became the 6th Baron Massy. John Thomas Massy was only 19yrs old when he inherited the Leitrim estates from his uncles and became a very rich young man. He continued to live in Co. Limerick and used Lareen as a sporting estate, letting Lareen House to sporting gentlemen. He also continued to expand his Leitrim landholdings, accumulating a total of 24,751 acres in the county. In 1875 he became a director of the newly established Sligo, Leitrim and Northern Counties Railway Company.

Hugh Hamon Ingoldsby, 5th Baron Massy of Duntrileague

Hugh Hamon Ingoldsby Massy, eldest son of the 4th Baron and Matilda White and elder brother of John Thomas Massy, was born on 14th April 1827, at Hermitage, Co. Limerick and succeeded his father as Baron at the age of 9yrs. Until he reached the age of 21 years in 1848, the landholdings of Lord Massy were effectively managed by his mother Matilda, Dowager Baroness Massy (Luke White's daughter) through the family Trustees. In 1850 the 5th Baron purchased Milford House on the banks of the Shannon River at Castletroy, Co. Limerick, from the Maunsell family. Milford House is located a few miles down river from Hermitage. His mother the Dowager Lady Matilda Massy resided at Milford House from 1850 until her death in 1883. Hugh Hamon Ingoldsby, 5th Baron Massy married Isabella Nesbitt of Cairnhill, Lanarkshire on 4th January 1855 at Charlotte Square, Edinburgh, and died without issue on 27th February 1874, aged 46, at 12 Atholl Crescent, Edinburgh.

The following report appeared in the Irish Times of February 28th 1874:-

DEATH OF LORD MASSY

A telegram received in Limerick today announces the death of Lord Massy of the Hermitage, Castleconnell at the age of forty-seven. The deceased nobleman had been in delicate health for some years and a constant anxiety to his friends. The Hon. John Thomas William Massy succeeds to the title. The deceased nobleman, Hugh Hamon Ingoldsby Massy, was the fifth baron of the name. He married on 5th June 1853, Isabella, daughter of the late George Moors Nesbitt of Cairn Hill. The present Lord is married to a daughter of the third Earl of Carrick.

His wife, Lady Isabella Massy, retired to live in London where she died on 27th July 1917. Her remains are interred in the Charnel House at Duntrileague.

John Thomas William, 6th Baron Massy of Duntrileague

John Thomas William Massy, brother of the 5th Baron, was born on 30th August 1835 and was just one year old when his father, the 4th Baron died on 27th September 1836. In 1854, at 19 years of age, he inherited Lareen House and over 20,000 acres of land in Leitrim from his uncles, Samuel and Luke White Jnr. who both died in that year. Appointed Sheriff of Co. Leitrim in 1863 and of Co. Limerick, 1873, he also served terms as Deputy Lieutenant of both counties. He married Lucy Maria Butler, daughter of the 3rd Earl of Carrick on 19th March 1863 at Mount Juliet, Co. Kilkenny and had one son, Hugh Somerset, and two daughters Lucy Matilda and Matilda Isabella. The 6th Baron's wife, Lady Lucy Maria Massy, died on 28th July 1896, aged 59, and is buried in the family vault at Castleconnell.

John Thomas, 6th Baron Massy
© *Guinness family collection*

John Thomas William Massy would not have anticipated his succession to the title, which occurred at the age of 38 following the death of his elder and only brother in 1874. He was by then a very rich man, having previously inherited the Leitrim estates from his uncles, Samuel and Luke White Jnr. He took his seat in Parliament as a Representative Peer (Conservative) in 1876. He died on 28th November 1915, aged 80, at Killakee, Co. Dublin. On 2nd December 1915, his remains were brought by train from Dublin to Castleconnell and following a funeral service in the local Church of Ireland parish church he was laid to rest in the Massy family vault alongside his wife and his mother.

The following obituary appeared in the Irish Times of Monday 29th November 1915.

LORD MASSY

We regret to announce that Lord Massy died at 5.15 o'clock yesterday afternoon at his residence, Killakee, Rathfarnham, County Dublin. He had been ill for some time, and his death was not unexpected.

John Thomas William Massy, D.L., J.P., Baron Massy, was the sixth holder of the title, the first baron's great grandfather, General Hugh Massy, having been one of the commanders sent to Ireland to suppress the rebellion of 1641. Since that period the family have been intimately associated with the social and public life of the counties of Limerick and Tipperary. John Thomas William, Baron Massy was born on the 30th August 1835, being the second son of the fourth Baron Massy and the daughter of Luke White, of Woodlands, Co. Dublin. He succeeded his elder brother, Hugh Hamon Ingoldsby, fifth baron, who died without issue, on 27th February 1874, and has been a representative Peer for Ireland since 1876. He married Lady Lucy Maria Butler, daughter of the third Earl of Carrick, in 1863, who died on the 25th July 1896, leaving one son and two daughters. He is succeeded in the title by his son, the Hon. Hugh Somerset John Massy. The late Lord Massy never took any particularly prominent part in the public or political life of Ireland. He was Sheriff for County Leitrim for 1863 and for County Limerick for 1873. He only occasionally attended the House of Lords, and very seldom intervened in the debates.

His whole life was devoted to the welfare of his tenants, who, one and all, held him in terms of affectionate regard. He was one of the real old-style sportsmen, and always took a deep personal interest in the work of the Irish Game Protection Association, and presided at all its annual meetings during the past ten or twelve years. He was indefatigable in looking after the interests of the Association in London when there were Parliamentary discussions on the administration of the Game and Inland Revenue Laws in Ireland. He was never happier than when surrounded by a circle of his chosen sportsmen friends, and many happy reunions took place at his annual "shoots" on the preserve attached to his estate at Killakee, Rathfarnham. He invariably resided at the Hermitage, Castleconnell during the spring and summer months, and was one of the most distinguished salmon fishermen on this important reach of the Shannon. His hospitality here was unbounded, and it was largely due to his interest that Castleconnell became so deservedly popular as a fishing centre.

It was during the tenure of the 6th Baron that the wealth of the Massy family reached its peak, and, ironically, it was also during his tenure that the seeds of the subsequent catastrophic collapse in the family's fortunes were sown. To understand how this collapse came about it is necessary to have a general appreciation of the factors that led to the decline of landed estates in Ireland.

Decline of Landed Estates in Ireland

Following the confiscation and reallocation of Catholic landholdings under Cromwell, over 90% of Irish landholdings came into the ownership of Protestant landlords, approximately one-third of whom were absentee landlords. Grants of land in Ireland were sometimes accompanied by a peerage. The Protestant holders of Irish landed estates became known under the collective term, the Ascendancy. By 1700 there were some 8,000 Protestant landholders (i.e. with landholdings over 500 acres) in Ireland. For just over one hundred years after the defeat of James II at the Battle of the Boyne in 1690, the Protestant Ascendancy ruled Ireland without any opposition. They had their own parliament and university in Dublin.

They held all of the offices of government and the judiciary, both national and local. Penal laws were introduced to suppress the influence of the Catholic Church, and the Church of Ireland became the established church. A large military force, deployed throughout the country, ensured the reluctant compliance of the Catholic population.

The success of the American War of Independence in 1776 and the French Revolution of 1789 had a significant impact on the mood of the Catholic population in Ireland. The outbreak of widespread rebellion in 1798, although ruthlessly suppressed, unnerved Ascendancy Ireland, and was a precursor to a series of events which would lead, in time, to the total collapse of Ascendancy rule in Ireland. Within two years of the 1798 rebellion, the Irish parliament was dissolved and political power transferred to Westminster. In 1829 the Catholic Emancipation Bill was passed leading to a resurgence of the Catholic Church in Ireland.

The Irish Famine, which began in 1845, impacted on the Ascendancy in different ways. For most landowners there was a substantial drop in rental income forcing them to borrow to maintain their properties and lifestyle. Some landowners took the opportunity to clear their estates of overcrowded tenantry, sometimes paying their fares to other countries. Between 1846 and 1853 approximately 70,000 tenant families were evicted. To their credit, some landowners impoverished themselves trying to help their destitute tenants. At the onset of the Famine, the 5th Baron Massy was a minor and his affairs were being managed by his mother. There is no record of Lady Matilda Massy being involved in tenant evictions. By the end of the Famine the number of landed proprietors had decreased to approx. 6,500. The post-Famine period 1854–1877 saw a substantial improvement in agricultural output and estate incomes. Many landlords, unwisely, borrowed heavily during this period to enlarge their houses, buy works of art and enhance their demesnes and gardens. It was a decision that they would come to regret, and pay dearly for, in subsequent years. Money was also regularly borrowed to cover the cost of marriage and other settlements on family members. Repayment of these loans was almost totally dependent on rental income from tenants.

A prolonged period of agricultural depression began in 1877 which, unfortunately for landowners, coincided with the growth of the Land

League led by Michael Davitt, which initiated a successful campaign of agitation for substantial reductions in tenant rents. Many tenants withheld rents and landlords were forced to concede substantial rent reductions. The combined impact of the agricultural depression and the reduction in rental income obliged landlords to resort to increased bank borrowings to maintain their lifestyle. Some landowners even borrowed money to pay the interest due on previous loans. The Land League allied itself with the Irish Party, which under Charles Stuart Parnell became a powerful advocate of Ireland's interests within the British Parliament. The Liberal British Prime Minister, William Ewart Gladstone, whose liberal principles were grounded in a Christian sense of justice, became an unlikely champion of the Irish cause. In 1869 his Liberal government disestablished the Church of Ireland, and in 1870 he introduced a Land Act which eased the conditions of tenants on Irish estates. From 1881 onwards Gladstone introduced a series of Irish Land Acts which facilitated the purchase of landholdings by tenants. However it was the Wyndham Land Act of 1903, which gave landowners a 12% bonus payment in addition to a purchase price of 18 times annual rent, that led to a massive transfer of land to tenants.

In the summer of 1892, alarmed at the wider implications of the Land Acts and the campaign for Home Rule on the future of the Ascendancy in Ireland, a great Unionist convention was held in Dublin in an unsuccessful effort to safeguard their position. The delegates filled two halls; in the larger of the two, the chairman, Lord Fingall, was supported by more than a hundred other notabilities, including the Duke of Leinster, Lords Mayo, Dunsany, Emly, Ventry, Massy and Cloncurry.

The First World War had a further devastating impact on Ascendancy life with many of the younger male generation being killed or maimed. By the time that the Irish Free State was established in 1922 most of the landed estates were either gone or in serious decline. The introduction of the Free State Land Act of 1923 with its provision for compulsory purchase of estate lands to relieve land congestion dealt a further blow to the continuation of the Ascendancy lifestyle.

Descendants of Captain Hugh Massy

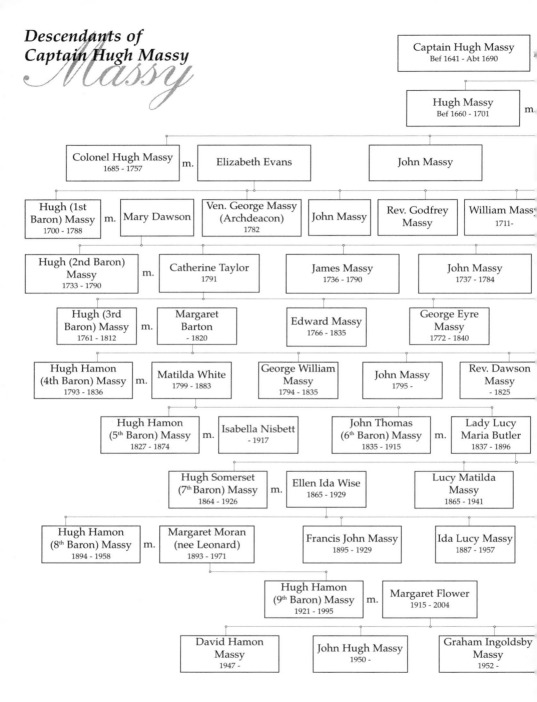

Captain Hugh Massy
Bef 1641 - Abt 1690

Hugh Massy
Bef 1660 - 1701 — m.

Colonel Hugh Massy
1685 - 1757 — m. **Elizabeth Evans**

John Massy

Hugh (1st Baron) Massy
1700 - 1788 — m. **Mary Dawson**

Ven. George Massy (Archdeacon)
1782

John Massy

Rev. Godfrey Massy

William Massy
1711-

Hugh (2nd Baron) Massy
1733 - 1790 — m. **Catherine Taylor**
1791

James Massy
1736 - 1790

John Massy
1737 - 1784

Hugh (3rd Baron) Massy
1761 - 1812 — m. **Margaret Barton**
- 1820

Edward Massy
1766 - 1835

George Eyre Massy
1772 - 1840

Hugh Hamon (4th Baron) Massy
1793 - 1836 — m. **Matilda White**
1799 - 1883

George William Massy
1794 - 1835

John Massy
1795 -

Rev. Dawson Massy
- 1825

Hugh Hamon (5th Baron) Massy
1827 - 1874 — m. **Isabella Nisbett**
- 1917

John Thomas (6th Baron) Massy
1835 - 1915 — m. **Lady Lucy Maria Butler**
1837 - 1896

Hugh Somerset (7th Baron) Massy
1864 - 1926 — m. **Ellen Ida Wise**
1865 - 1929

Lucy Matilda Massy
1865 - 1941

Hugh Hamon (8th Baron) Massy
1894 - 1958 — m. **Margaret Moran (nee Leonard)**
1893 - 1971

Francis John Massy
1895 - 1929

Ida Lucy Massy
1887 - 1957

Hugh Hamon (9th Baron) Massy
1921 - 1995 — m. **Margaret Flower**
1915 - 2004

David Hamon Massy
1947 -

John Hugh Massy
1950 -

Graham Ingoldsby Massy
1952 -

Margaret Percy

Amy Benson

Alice Massy

William Massy
- 1768

Rev. Charles Massy

Margaret Massy

Amy Massy

Eyre Massy (1st
Baron Clarina)

Charles Massy

Mary
Massy

Amy Massy

Elizabeth
Massy

Catherine
Massy

Elizabeth Massy

John Massy
- 1869

Mary Anne
Massy

Catherine
Massy

Jane Massy

Sarah Massy

Grace Elizabeth
Massy
- 1841

Cathenne
Massy
- 1847

Susan Maria
Massy

Margaret
Everina Massy
- 1885

Elizabeth Jane
Massy
- 1874

Matilda Isabella
Massy
1867 -

Muriel Olive
Massy
1892 - Abt 1990

Daughter
Massy
1893 - 1893

Lillian Ierne
Massy
1897 - Bef 1990

Paul Robert
Massy
1953

Sheelagh Marie
Massy
1958 -

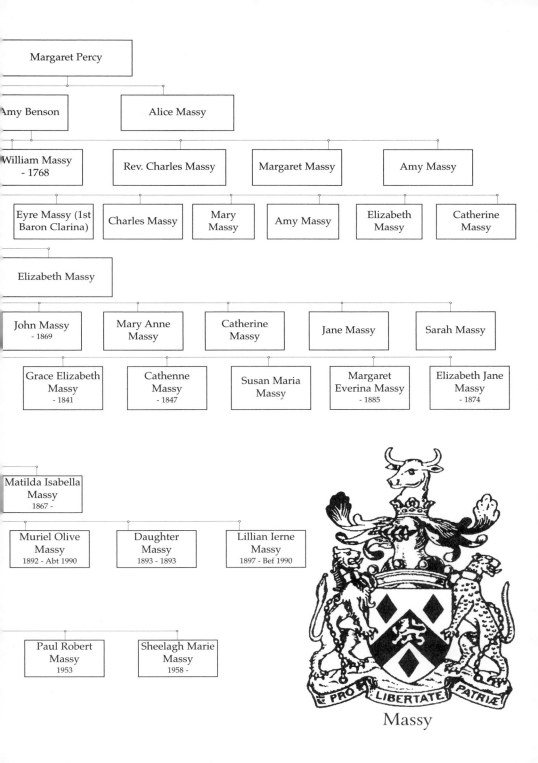

Massy

It was essential that the money that landlords received from the sale of their landholdings under the Land Acts be wisely invested. Even then, the income from those investments was, in almost all instances, insufficient to sustain the large houses, demesnes and lavish lifestyles of the landlords. Many landlords lost substantial amounts of money on poorly judged investments. Some merely treated the money from land sales as income and spent it, with inevitable and disastrous consequences for their descendants. The more perceptive landlords grasped that the privileged position of the Protestant Ascendancy in Ireland was over and was being rapidly overtaken by social and political revolution. They sold their landholdings, disposed of their mansions, sometimes by simply abandoning them, adjusted their lifestyle, and invested heavily in the education of their children in the professions of education, law, architecture, engineering and medicine. Some Ascendancy families simply sold off their estates and emigrated to England or other parts of the British Empire.

The Protestant Ascendancy in Ireland was noted for beautiful demesnes, magnificent houses and gardens, and extravagant lifestyles that were almost totally dependent on rents collected from tenant farmers on their estates. The overwhelmingly Catholic population of the country, which saw the Ascendancy as imposed, self-interested rentiers, never accepted the legitimacy of their dominant status, and were always prone to acts of rebellion. Because of their extravagant lifestyle, and its effect on the Catholic population, there has been a tendency to portray the impact of the Protestant Ascendancy on Irish history as wholly negative. It is, however, one of the great paradoxes of Irish history that the Protestant Ascendancy also produced such people as Isaac Butt, Henry Grattan, Thomas Davis, Robert Emmett, Theobald Wolfe Tone, Lord Edward Fitzgerald, Charles Stuart Parnell, Roger Casement, Countess Markiewicz, Robert Barton and many others who played significant roles in promoting the cause of political independence even, in some cases, at the cost of their own lives. The Protestant Ascendancy also produced such literary and cultural luminaries as Jonathan Swift, Edmund Burke, Oliver Goldsmith, Oscar Wilde, Percy French, Samuel Ferguson, William Butler Yeats, Jack Yeats, George Bernard Shaw, John Millington Synge, Lady

Augusta Gregory, Elizabeth Bowen and William Orpen. The foundation of the Gaelic League was in large measure due to the determined efforts of enlightened members of Ascendancy families. The first President of Ireland, Douglas Hyde, and the fourth President, Erskine Childers were both from Ascendancy families.

Many children of Ascendancy families went on as adults to make a very real and meaningful contribution to the social, cultural and economic development of the Irish State that emerged after the Treaty of 1922.

Today, the scattered remnants of the Protestant Ascendancy in Ireland are, in the words of the author Evelyn Waugh, *"quietly receding into their own mist."*

Annie Massy

Annie Letitia Massy was born in 1867, the third child of Hugh and Anne Massy of Stagdale Lodge Co. Tipperary. A shy child, Annie developed a lifelong interest in birds, fish and flowers. In 1885 while living at Coolakeigh, Enniskerry, Co. Wicklow, Annie observed a pair of redstarts nesting at Deerpark on Lord Powerscourt's Estate. Her observation of the first known Irish nesting redstarts was verified by an eminent ornithologist, Rev. Charles William Benson. Annie was a regular contributor to the Irish Naturalist in which journal she gave regular accounts of her many finds and observations. In 1901 she was employed in the biology section of the fisheries division in the newly established Department of Agriculture. She moved residence at this time to Malahide on the north Co. Dublin coast where she could be regularly observed studying marine life and shells along the shoreline. She developed a particular interest and expertise in molluscs and in 1907 she published her first major scientific paper in which she identified a number of new species of cephalopods. This was to be the first of many exceptional papers by Annie on marine biology. In time she became recognised as an international expert in the classification of molluscs. It was an extraordinary achievement for a person with no formal scientific education.

In 1904 she was one of the founders of the Irish Society for the Protection of Birds, the forerunner of the present day Irish Wildbird Conservancy. She maintained a lifelong interest in the study of bird life. In the early 1920s she moved from Malahide to Howth where she lived at her home, 'Galteemore', until her death. In 1926 the Society for the Protection of Birds was on the point of dissolution when Annie, the only surviving founder member, volunteered to take over as honorary secretary to keep the society going. This revived the society and it went on to open up the valuable field of bird-protection work in the new Free State, culminating in the Wild Birds Protection Act of 1930. The Irish Times noted that Miss Massy, while modestly keeping herself in the background, worked untiringly for the society. She remained a committed secretary to the society until her death. Annie Letitia Massy, distinguished naturalist, marine biologist and international expert on molluscs died, aged 64, on 6 April 1931. In an obituary, the journal Nature said "Her death, unexpected and all too soon, takes away a careful, critical, and efficient though retiring zoologist with no ambition but to do her work thoroughly, and a valued friend to all who knew her." The Irish Naturalists Journal said, *even the ravens will miss her.*" She is buried in St Andrew's Churchyard in Malahide, Co. Dublin and it is said that, in a moment of stillness at her funeral, a robin began to sing. (Summarised from an article by Anne Byrne)

Demise of Lord Massy's Estates

In 1878 the total landholdings of the extended Massy/Massey families in Ireland amounted to over 98,000 acres. The landholdings of John Thomas, 6th Baron Massy consisted of 8,568 acres in Co. Limerick, 24,751 acres in Co. Leitrim (acquired through the Whites), and 1,120 acres in Co. Tipperary, a total of 34,439 acres. The estate at Killakee was, at that time, still in the registered ownership of Mrs. Anne Salisbury White, Samuel White's widow. Mrs White died on 27th November 1880 and in her will she left Killakee House and 3,422 acres, including the magnificent gardens, to her late husband's nephew, John Thomas, 6th Baron Massy. Her sister-in-law, the Dowager Baroness Lady Matilda Massy (Luke White's daughter, and mother of the 6th Baron) died at her home, Milford

House, County Limerick, on 27th February 1883, aged 84, and is buried in the family vault at Castleconnell. Following her death, the 6th Baron sold Milford House to Mr Edmund Maglin Russell, a wealthy merchant whose family had a long association with civic life in Limerick. At one time they owned the largest milling industry in Ireland. The Russell mills were subsequently purchased by Messrs. Ranks (Ireland) Ltd. The Russell's sold Milford House to a religious order, the Little Company of Mary, in 1923. The Little Company of Mary now provides a hospice care centre at Milford House for people with terminal illness.

In 1878 a wall was built by the 6th Baron from behind the hill at the rear of Massy Lodge to the western slopes of Galtymore Mountain. It took 30-40 men four years to build and acted as a boundary between the estates of Galtee Castle and the Massy estates. The main reason for building the wall was to give employment to local small farmers during a period of economic depression. The wall covers several of the main peaks of the Galtees and ninety per cent of it still stands.

The landholdings and other properties of Lord Massy were vested in a trusteeship that was established to minimise tax liabilities and death duties, and to ensure the effective transfer of the estate from one generation to another. Each Baron had the use of the land and properties for his lifetime and any borrowings or sale of land/properties required the agreement of the trustees. The trustees of the Massy estate were the family's legal representatives. Each Baron, during his lifetime, lived off the rental income from tenanted landholdings. The rental income from the 6th Baron's tenanted landholdings is estimated to have peaked at around £12,101 per annum in 1881 (approximately €1,050,000 in present-day values), a very considerable sum of money for that time. However following a national campaign of agitation by tenants for fairer rents throughout the 1880s and a prolonged agricultural depression which began in 1877, rental income on landed estates declined significantly.

The tenanted landholdings of Lord Massy were disposed of under the terms of the Settled Land Act (1882), the Ashbourne Land Act (1885) and the Balfour Land Act (1891). Unfortunately these sales occurred during a period of agricultural depression and the terms were not particularly attractive for landlords. It is not possible to accurately state how much money was received from the sale of the Massy landholdings, as the relevant Land Commission files are not yet available for public examination. However, on the basis of the known terms of the Land Acts, and the declining value of land, it is likely that a sum of around £90,000 (approximately €8,000,000 in present-day values) was received. If Lord Massy had held off selling his tenanted landholdings until the Wyndham Land Act of 1903 he would have had the benefit of continued rental income up to 1903 and been assured of a sale price of 18 times the annual rent plus a 12% cash bonus i.e £151,000 (a total of €13,500,000 approx in present day values).

It is not clear as to why the 6th Baron decided to sell the Massy landholdings when he did. Perhaps it was a reaction to the national campaign of tenant agitation. An incident that occurred at Lord Massy's Lodge near Anglesboro in 1881 is a good indicator of the level of tension that existed between landlords and tenants at the time.

Siege of Massy Lodge

On 12th August 1881 a group of troops accompanied by a son of Lord Massy's agent, Mr. Townsend, repaired to Massy Lodge to wine and dine for the night after a successful day's grouse shooting. In the middle of the night the revellers were awoken by loud voices. Rushing to the windows, they observed a large threatening crowd outside led by a local land league activist, Willie Condon. They took up arms to defend themselves. Eventually, however, the crowd dispersed and as dawn broke the shooting party endeavoured to quietly leave the Lodge and make for the safety of the police barracks in Kilfinane. To their horror, they found that their horses had been released and dispersed into the surrounding woods. They were trapped in Massy Lodge. Eventually, some two days later, a contingent of thirty troops was despatched from Kilfinane to rescue the shooting party. As the troops passed through Ballylanders, crowds' gathered and chapel bells rang out. A few miles from Anglesboro they were forced to a halt by a substantial wall built across the roadway. Having cleared a passage they moved on, but after some time encountered another wall that had to be cleared. Within a quarter mile of the Lodge gate they were confronted by yet another wall. As they moved along the driveway to the Lodge they found their way blocked by a number of large trees lying across the driveway. Having eventually reached Massy Lodge and rescued the shooting party, the entire contingent set out for Kilfinane. On the return journey they again had to deal with a series of road blockages. The authorities were so alarmed by this incident that they billeted sixty members of the Royal Irish Constabulary in Massy Lodge. Local farms were raided and a large number of cattle were confiscated and held in the village of Anglesboro, to be sold off or returned to their owners, if they were willing to pay for them. Several hundred cattle were seized during the raids, which lasted six days. Each evening the police and military retired to Massy Lodge to wine and dine at a large bonfire in front of the house.

The 6th Baron's lifestyle

John Thomas, 6th Baron Massy was a very strong willed person who took to the baronial lifestyle with relish, lived life to the full and became famous for hosting shooting parties at Killakee, and fishing parties at Hermitage. He was a member of the Kildare Street Club in Dublin, the Carlton Club in London, and of the Limerick Hunt. He was also a founder member and patron of the Irish Game Protection Association. Lord Massy maintained a large fleet of horse-drawn carriages of various types at Killakee, which were used for collecting his guests in Dublin and also for transporting them on shooting expeditions in the Dublin Mountains. Large dining shelters would be set up in the woods, where shooting parties would adjourn for lunch. Tables would be laid out in these shelters with the finest tableware, and food would be transported in pony carts from Killakee House. Lord Massy kept a record in two game registers of shooting parties in which he participated. These registers cover the period from 1886 to 1915, the year of his death. They show that he participated in shooting parties, not only as host at Killakee, but also

Life at Killakee
© Guinness family collection

on estates all over Ireland. The list of participants on these shooting parties is a veritable who's who of ascendancy Ireland. From mid-August until mid-December each year Lord Massy hosted a series of shooting parties at Killakee. Each shooting party consisted of up to 16 people and they would each spend a number of days shooting game mainly on Glendoo (Gleann Dubh - Black Glen) and Cruagh (Creebheach – Bushy Land) mountains and in the Killakee woodlands. The main species of game were grouse, woodcock, snipe, rabbits and hares. After each day's shooting, guests and their companions would enjoy the hospitality of Lord Massy at Killakee House. The task of accommodating guests and their servants at Killakee was a mammoth organisational operation, which required a small army of staff ranging from coachmen, stablemen, house servants, gardeners, cooks, and gamekeepers. In the early nineteen hundreds men were paid four shillings a day by Lord Massy as ground beaters on grouse drives in the Dublin Mountains. This was very good wages at the time. During the shooting season Lord Massy also participated in shooting parties on many other estates throughout Ireland, all of which are recorded in his game registers. Foremost among the estates he regularly visited were Tibradden, Powerscourt, Luggala, Glenarm, Glenstal, Elm Park, Glenfarne, Straffan, Lough Rynn, Carriglass, Parlington, Moore Abbey, Woodlawn, Garvald, Kilboy, Clonbrock, Moydrum, Dromoland Castle, Birr Castle, Grantston Manor, Larsden, Brown's Bank, Wintermuir, Castlegar, and French Park. The number of shooting parties dropped dramatically on the outset of the First World War in 1914. The last shooting party in which Lord Massy participated was at Elm Park on January 8th 1915, ten months before he died. The last game shoots recorded in Lord Massy's game book for Killakee were 11th September, 1915 when Major E.H. Guinness of Tibradden shot 6 grouse and one hare, and 21st October, 1915 when Mr S.C. Vansittart, Lord Massy's son-in-law, shot 2 woodcock. The last insert in the game book is a letter of sympathy on his death to his daughter Mrs. Lucy Matilda Guinness from the Irish Game Protection Association.

Killakee was also a regular venue for house parties, particularly during Punchestown races, the Dublin Horse Show and the Dublin Castle Season. It is said that on the occasion of house parties at Killakee, long lines of guests' carriages could be seen stretched along the main avenue to the house. Family life alternated between Killakee for the shooting season and Hermitage for the fishing season, involving a mass movement of family members and house-servants between the two locations. A large complement of outdoor staff was employed at both demesnes to maintain the gardens. Lord Massy held the fishing rights on a stretch of the Shannon River at Castleconnell which, at that time, was one of the premier salmon fishing rivers in Europe. During the fishing season salmon could be seen in their thousands lining up to ascend the rapids at Castleconnell. There was a local saying that *"a person could cross the Shannon at Castleconnell by walking on the backs of the salmon."* Alas, that is not the case today. A combination of the impact of the Shannon Hydroelectric Scheme, agricultural/ industrial pollution of the river, and the world-wide depletion of salmon stocks through overfishing has had a drastic impact on fish levels in the river. He also held fishing rights on Lough Melvin and the Drowes River in Co. Leitrim, which to this day is one of the finest locations for salmon fishing in Europe. Lord Massy maintained a register of salmon caught at Hermitage, part of which i.e. from 1906 onwards, has survived. This register shows that Lord Massy and his guests spent the months of May, June and July each year salmon fishing on the Shannon River at Hermitage. The weights of many of the recorded catches are by current standards quite phenomenal.

At the time of the land sale Lord Massy had, not only a large mansion and demesne at Hermitage, but also at Lareen in Co. Leitrim. He had also just inherited Killakee House and demesne, and he owned Massy Lodge in Co. Limerick. In addition his extended family was dependent on the family trusteeship for their incomes. There was no way that the running costs of these properties and the maintenance of the family's lifestyle could be sustained by the income from investment of the land settlement monies. There is no record of any profitable investments of the Massy land settlement monies. It would appear that while some investments were made, they were not profitable. An investment of £10,500 in the Sligo-Leitrim and Northern Counties Railway Company of which Lord Massy was a director, for example, never produced a dividend and was worth a mere £131-7s-6d at the time of the 6th Baron's death. Lord Massy

Weight 54 lbs
Length 50 Inches Girth 30 Inches

Life at Hermitage.
© *Guinness Family Collection*

used the land settlement monies to directly fund his lifestyle and provide an income for his family. It was therefore inevitable that this source of funding would eventually dry up. Had Lord Massy taken a decision to modify his lifestyle, and invest the bulk of the land settlement monies in more secure long-term investments and/or productive ventures he could have continued to live in comfort for his lifetime and also have laid a sound financial foundation for an ongoing source of supplementary income for future generations of his family.

It is clear that the extravagant lifestyle of the 6th Baron and the running costs of Hermitage, Killakee, Lareen and Massy Lodge were a very considerable drain on the family's declining financial resources. Ascendancy houses in Ireland were notoriously expensive to run and maintain. Many landlords, however, were not prepared to compromise on their lifestyle, and it would appear that the 6th Baron Massy was included in their number. With little income of any significance from the few remaining tenants, or from investments, the only significant source of finance for the 6th Baron and his family was the land settlement monies. It does not appear to have occurred to him that curtailment of his lifestyle and a programme of prudent financial management was called for. On the contrary, his spending increased dramatically. He seems to have been either unaware or unconcerned about the implications of this spending for the wellbeing of future generations of his family. Perhaps he was aware, but did not face up to the long-term consequences of his extravagant lifestyle. In any event, primary responsibility for the subsequent catastrophic collapse of the family's wealth rests with the 6th Baron and his extravagant lifestyle.

John Thomas Massy was always impeccably, and expensively, dressed and this emphasis on good dress extended to his staff. Family photographs show coachmen dressed in the finest livery, including top hats. He took eagerly to the introduction of the motor car, and his fleet included a motor charabanc for transporting shooting parties in the Dublin/Wicklow Mountains. Again, his chauffeurs were always smartly uniformed.

On the occasion of his 75th birthday in 1910 Lord Massy, in an interview with the Irish Times, expressed the view that the campaign for Home Rule in Ireland would inevitably lead to civil war. Five months after his death the 1916 Uprising took place in Dublin. The Uprising, and its aftermath, triggered a sequence of events that led to the establishment of the Irish Free State in 1922. While Lord Massy was correct in his forecast, and civil war did break out in Ireland, it was not for the reasons that he anticipated i.e. conflict between Nationalists and Unionists. The Irish Civil War, which broke out following the 1922 Anglo-Irish Treaty, was between differing factions of Nationalism.

The 6th Baron's tenure probably represents the zenith of the Massy dynasty in terms of the lifestyle enjoyed by himself and his family. During his lifetime he inherited over 34,000 acres of land, three mansions and demesnes at Hermitage, Killakee and Lareen, and a summer home, Massy Lodge, in the foothills of the Galtee Mountains. Massy Lodge and some 160 acres of land was sold by the family trustees in 1913 for £1,300 to a Mr John Hanley who had returned from Australia to settle in Ireland. Massy Lodge is still in the ownership of the Hanley family. The 6th Baron sold Lareen, including a demesne of 152 acres, in 1912 to Maxwell Vandalear Blacker-Douglas for £3,500. Included in the sale was *"the bed and soil of Lough Melvin and the waters thereof.....to pass and re-pass the banks of the lake...for fishing."* The sale of these properties is a clear indication that the family's financial position was coming under increasing pressure towards the end of the 6th Baron's life.

By the time he died on 28th November 1915, the estate was hopelessly in debt to the bank. In his will, which he made in July 1915, he left large amounts of silver plate to his two daughters, Lucy Matilda Guinness and Matilda Isabella Vansittart. He left his hunting guns and fishing rods to his eldest grandson, Hugh Hamon. He also left substantial amounts of family jewellery in trust to Hugh Hamon. Interestingly, he left nothing from his personal estate to his son, Hugh Somerset, who is not mentioned in the will. It is noticeable from reading the 6th Baron's game registers that whereas up to 1893 his son, Hugh Somerset, participated in many of the shooting parties at Killakee, he does not feature at all in the list of participants after that date. Neither does he feature in the entries in the fishing register at Hermitage. It is reputed that there was a strained relationship between the 6th Baron and the family of his son's wife, the Wises of Rochestown. This may have affected the relationship between the 6th Baron and his son. In any event, there is no indication that the Wises participated in shooting parties at Killakee or fishing at Hermitage. His will states that in the event of there being any residue from his personal estate, after payment of debts, it is to be divided between his two daughters. The will gives the family trustees full responsibility for any actions necessary to settle outstanding debts. Following his death it was confirmed that the family trusteeship was hopelessly indebted to the bank.

Hermitage Auction

In January 1916, less than two months after the 6th Baron's death, the entire contents of the Hermitage mansion were sold by the Trustees to meet his outstanding debts. The auction took place on 20/21 and 24/25 January. A catalogue produced by Wm. B. Fitt Auctioneers of Limerick lists almost 900 lots. The first three days of the auction consisted of a systematic, room by room sale of the house contents. The final day consisted of a sale of horses and outdoor goods e.g. horse carriages, equestrian tackle, plants from the glasshouses and fruit from the orchards. Many of the family's more valuable heirlooms were transferred to Killakee House. All that was left at

© National Library of Ireland

Hermitage was an empty, uninhabited mansion. Efforts to sell the Hermitage mansion failed. The First World War was raging in Europe, Ascendancy life in Ireland was in decline, and there simply was neither the market nor the money for large country houses such as Hermitage.

Five months after the 6th Baron's death the Easter Rebellion took place in Dublin leading to the Irish War of Independence, which changed the political landscape of Ireland forever. John Thomas Massy had the good fortune to have inherited the peerage at a time of great fortune for the Massy family, and the good luck to die, after a long and privileged life, five months before the republican rebellion of 1916.

Hugh Somerset Massy, 7th Baron Massy of Duntrileague

Hugh Somerset Massy, only son of the 6th Baron and Lucy Maria Butler, was born on 15th February 1864. He served as Lieutenant in the 5th Battalion, Leinster Regiment 1881-1885 and was appointed High Sheriff of Co. Limerick in 1887. He married Ellen Ida Wise of Rochestown Co. Tipperary on 16th September 1886 and set up his residence at Ardfinnan House, a moderately sized Glebe house close to the Wise estate at Rochestown. The couple had two sons, Hugh Hamon and Francis John, and three daughters Ida Lucy, Muriel Olive and Lillian Ierne. Hugh Somerset Massy had a good relationship with his father up to about 1893, after which the relationship appears to have deteriorated. He succeeded to the title, at the age of fifty-one, in November 1915 on the death of his father. The 7th Baron inherited a truly appalling situation. There were two demesnes with large mansions and gardens to be maintained at Hermitage and Killakee, together with his own house at Ardfinnan, Co. Tipperary. The magnificent Killakee gardens alone required a small army of gardeners and outdoor workers, and considerable financial expenditure to maintain. With the tenanted landholdings

Ardfinnan House
© *English family collection*

sold off, there simply was no ongoing source of income to meet all of these demands. In addition there was the burden of servicing accumulated bank debts, the extent of which only became apparent after his father's death. A major programme of retrenchment was embarked upon in an attempt to contain the situation. Unable to afford the cost of maintaining two large mansions, Lord Massy remained living at Ardfinnan House with a staff of three, a butler, a maid and a cook. The indoor and outdoor staff at Hermitage and Killakee House were discharged.

Hugh Hamon Charles Massy (*future 8th Baron Massy*)

Lord and Lady Massy now faced another very serious crisis, and from a totally unanticipated source. Their eldest son and heir, Hugh Hamon Charles George, was born at Ardfinnan House on 13th July 1894. He had an idyllic childhood amid the grandeur and excitement of life on his grandfather's estates. His grandfather's game register for Killakee shows that the young Hamon Massy participated in shooting parties as a boy while on holidays from school at Harrow and later as a young man. He grew up with the expectation that, one-day, all of his grandfather's apparent wealth would pass to him as the 8th Baron Massy. It is known that the 6th Baron was genuinely fond of his grandchildren.

The young Hamon Massy was prone to occasional episodes of ill health, which possibly explains his non-enlistment, unlike his younger brother Francis, for military service in the First World War. Following his grandfather's death, Hamon Massy took up residence in Killakee House. He lived the life of an unattached gentleman, attending social events and driving around in the last remaining of his grandfather's motor cars. He inherited his grandfather's liking for smart cloths and was always well dressed. He was a handsome, well-spoken young man. Unfortunately, however, he had developed an early liking for alcohol, assisted it is believed by a misguided family butler. In his mid-twenties he was hospitalised for a period of time in Mercer's Hospital, Dublin. While there, he became friendly with a nurse, Margaret Moran, second daughter of Richard Leonard and Mary Greene of Meadsbrook, Ashbourne, Co.

Meath, and widow of a Dr. Moran of Tara, Co. Meath, by whom she had three infant children, a daughter Ethel and twins Maureen and Desmond. The friendship blossomed into romance and, in 1918, Hamon Massy informed his family of his intention to marry Margaret Moran. This announcement caused considerable, and understandable, disquiet to his parents. The family had disposed of their tenanted landholdings, the 6th Baron had effectively squandered the family fortune, the family had an appalling level of debt, the country was in the throes of a republican rebellion against the Crown, the son and heir to the Massy title had a serious drink problem, and he now proposed to marry a Catholic. This proposal threatened the very foundations of the family.

Under the strictly enforced rules of the Catholic Church, pressure would undoubtedly be brought to bear to have any children from the marriage raised as Catholics. This prospect presented the Massy family with, what was for them, an unacceptable prospect. The stability and status of the Protestant Ascendancy rested on three foundational pillars, land ownership, allegiance to the Crown, and the Protestant faith. For the Massy family, all three pillars were now collapsing around them.

Hamon Massy stood his ground and on January 2nd 1919 he married Margaret Moran in a Roman Catholic ceremony at University Church, St. Stephen's Green Dublin. He was 25yrs old and she was 26.The witnesses to the marriage were Hamon's sister, Lillian, and Margaret Moran's sister May Leonard. The entry in the marriage register in University Church contains an additional

Pictorial Record of Irish Events

The Hon. Hamon Massy.　　Mrs. Margaret Moran.

Were married last week at the University Church, St. Stephen's Green. Mr. Massy is the eldest son of Lord Massy, Castleconnell, and resides at Killakee. The bride is the widow of the late Dr. Moran, Tara, and a daughter of the late Richard Leonard and Mrs. Leonard, Moundsbrook, Ashbourne.

© *Irish Independent*

note by the officiating priest to the effect that Hamon Massy was a convert to Catholicism. Following the marriage, Hamon Massy and his wife took up residence at Killakee House.

Margaret Massy was a staunch Catholic who was assiduous in the practice of her religion. The Massy family, for its part, was staunchly Protestant. The 1901 and 1911 census returns, for example, show that all the house servants at Killakee and the Hermitage were of the Protestant persuasion. The marriage of Hamon Massy and Margaret Moran was not approved by Lord and Lady Massy and caused a serious, and permanent, rift between Hamon Massy and his parents.

Killakee Auction

By mid-1919 the family's financial situation was extremely grim with large debts still outstanding from the 6th Baron's time. The trustees were obliged to sell off cherished family heirlooms to meet these outstanding and accumulating debts. A catalogue of Bennett and Son, Auctioneers, shows that in July 1919 " by direction of the Trustees of the late Lord Massy", huge quantities of silver plate; jewellery; old cut glass; Worcester, Staffordshire, Minton and Dresden china; Sheraton and Chippendale furniture; and a large art collection including works by Giotto, Carpaccio, Raphael and Osborne were sold in an auction that lasted several days. The timing of the auction of the Massy heirlooms, although absolutely necessary, was particularly unfortunate. In 1919 Ireland was in the throes of armed insurrection and the British economy was experiencing a period of post-war depression. In these circumstances it was a

CATALOGUE

OF

Old English & Irish Silver

Important Jewels, Sheffield Plate Decorative Furniture, Porcelain Old Glass, Oil Paintings Drawings, Engravings, and other Works of Art.

To be Sold by Auction

(By direction of the Trustees of the late LORD MASSY, and for other accounts).

At the Galleries, 6 Upper Ormond Quay,

On Tuesday, the 8th of July, 1919,

AND FOLLOWING DAYS,

Commencing at Twelve o'clock, Noon.

ON VIEW THE DAY PRECEDING.

BENNETT & SON,

Auctioneers and Valuers,

6 UPPER ORMOND QUAY, DUBLIN.

© National Library of Ireland

buyers market and most of the valuable artefacts were sold for far less than their real value.

Burning of Hermitage

The political situation in Ireland for the Ascendancy was also becoming increasingly ominous. Following the 1916 Rising, the Sinn Féin movement emerged, grew in strength and developed a military wing. The aspiration of the majority of Irish people shifted from Home Rule to full independence. A ruthless guerrilla war was being waged against British rule. 1920 was a particularly tense year. Servants of the Crown were under daily fear for their lives, and many were killed. The number of Magistrates, Police and other public servants resigning their posts developed into a flood. Burning of police barracks became a regular occurrence and many Ascendancy families sold up and moved residence to England. Large numbers of troop reinforcements were being brought into the country.

In February 1920, Summerhill House in Co. Meath became the first estate mansion to be burnt, apparently to prevent it being used for billeting troops. During the period 1920-22 some ninety-eight estate mansions were burned. These burnings took place primarily as reprisals for British troop actions, or to prevent mansions being used to billet troops. In the early hours of June 16th 1920 Hermitage was set on fire and burnt to the ground. Hermitage had been vacant since the death of the 6th Baron in 1915 and the contents had been sold off at the huge auction of January 1916. Hermitage was probably burnt because of a local rumour that it was going to be used to billet British troops.

The appalling catalogue of disasters that befell the family seems to have had an overwhelming impact on the 7th Baron's health. It would appear that he was simply unable to cope and took refuge in heavy drinking. From 1919 onwards all key actions affecting the family appear to have been taken by his wife, Lady Ellen Ida Massy. At the Limerick Quarter Sessions on 6th October 1920, Lady Massy submitted a claim for £70,000 compensation for the burning of the Hermitage mansion at Castleconnell. The case was adjourned for the purpose of valuation. At a subsequent sitting, Lady Massy obtained a decree for £28,500 and £609-7s-6d legal costs against Limerick Co. Council and Clare Co. Council, each of which was found liable for half of the award. Arising from the outcome of the 1918 elections most of the County Councils, including Limerick and Clare, had Sinn Féin majorities. The members of these Co. Councils refused to sanction payment of malicious damages awards to anyone associated with the British Establishment. The Massys were unable to obtain payment of the court decree.

On the 6th April 1921 Lady Massy applied to the Kings Bench Division for a conditional order against the Great Southern and Western Railway Co. for diversion to her, in part satisfaction of the decree, of £9,100 rates due by the Railway Company to Limerick Co. Council. Judge Samuels granted her the conditional order. The Railway Company, however, never paid the award and the incoming Free State government accepted no responsibility for payment of awards made before the Treaty. Around this time, Rochestown House, the home of Lady Massy's family, the Wises, was also burnt. Shortly afterwards, the head of the Wise family, Lady Massy's brother, Frank, took his own life.

Had Hermitage been burnt after the 1922 Treaty and during the ensuing Civil War the family would have fared better. Claims for compensation for houses burnt during the Civil War were dealt with by a special Commission set up by the Free State Government and compensation awards were paid by the Exchequer. The Massy family had the triple misfortune of selling their tenanted landholdings too early, being obliged to sell the family heirlooms at a time of economic depression and finally, of having their mansion at Castleconnell burnt down at the wrong time.

The apprehension of Lord and Lady Massy regarding the implications of their eldest son's marriage to Margaret Moran came to pass when a grandson and heir, **Hugh Hamon John Somerset**, was born at Killakee House on 11th June 1921 and baptised into the Roman Catholic Church.

Tragedy at Killakee

On the night of 19th July 1922, a day after the telephone wires to Killakee House had been cut and their car stolen, another event occurred which was to have a traumatic impact on Hamon Massy and his wife, and a fatal outcome for another man. According to Hamon Massy, he and his wife were in their bedroom, preparing for bed, when they heard footsteps on the gravel outside. Hamon opened the window and called out *"Hello, who is there?"* A man answered, saying that he wished to see him. He went downstairs, carrying a small hand lamp, as there was no electricity in the house, and let the man into the house. What happened next is not fully clear. It would appear that a noisy verbal altercation developed between the two men. Massy tried to get the man to leave the house and his wife, hearing the shouting, came downstairs and asked them not to awaken the baby. When the man refused to leave Massy, who had taken a revolver out of a drawer fired a shot over his head. The man caught hold of him. There was a struggle, another shot rang out, and the man fell mortally wounded. Massy was deeply distressed and he sent for the doctor and a priest. In the study, lit only by a small hand lamp, his wife prayed over the dying man. Hamon Massy was subsequently charged and acquitted of unlawfully killing of the man.

Death of Lady Ellen Ida Massy

Hamon Massy's mother, Lady Ellen Ida Constance Massy, wife of the 7th Baron, died suddenly on 15th January 1923 at the age of fifty-eight. She is buried in Ardfinnan churchyard. The untimely death of Lady Massy removed the only person in the family with the resolve to grapple with the family's rapidly deteriorating financial situation. She left financial settlements on her husband, second son and daughters, but excluded her eldest son, Hamon, from her will. These settlements were dependent on anticipated income from investment of the outstanding payment of compensation for the burning of Hermitage. As this compensation was never paid, the Massy family was now left without any source of income. The death of Lady Massy appears to have marked a turning point in the bank's attitude to the family's deepening financial crisis.

Killakee Eviction

As the family had no source of income to support their everyday living expenses, their financial position was desperate. Following the unexpected death of Lady Ellen Ida Massy, it became clear that the bank had no confidence in the capacity of either the 7th Baron or his son Hamon to deal with the family's financial problems. On 31st March 1924, the bankruptcy court granted a Dublin bank an order for possession of Killakee House. A temporary stay was put on execution of the order because Hamon Massy was ill and confined to bed. On Thursday 15th May 1924, however, an Under-Sheriff's Officer and two assistants arrived to take possession of Killakee House. Hamon Massy was unwell and in bed, but a doctor was called and he certified that he was fit to be moved. The officials sent for an ambulance, but he declined to get into it. He declared himself unable to walk and stated that the only way he would leave the house was to be carried out. The officials duly obliged, and he was lifted out of his bed by the Sheriff's men, carried along the upper driveway on his mattress and deposited on the nearby public roadway in front of a group of bemused locals who had gathered to witness the unfolding drama. He was 30 years old and the world, as he knew it, had come to a sudden and rather ignominious end. He remained on the roadway for a considerable time, comforted by his wife. Friends then took him and his wife in a private car to a city hotel. In an interview with reporters the following day, the Under-Sheriff, Mr. W. A. McCracken, solicitor, said; *"There have been no developments in the case, nor are any expected. The matter is an extremely delicate one and no useful purpose can be served by discussing it in the columns of the Press."* The incident was widely reported in the national newspapers.

The bank placed a caretaker in Killakee House. Mrs Massy and her infant son, Hughie, were given accommodation by Ms Margaret Fox in the nearby stewards house. Her charity did not extend to Hamon Massy. A local lady, Mrs Reid, subsequently gave Hamon Massy accommodation. The tenancy rights of tenants on the Killakee Demesne were not affected by the repossession. Hamon Massy and his family now had nowhere to live. By agreement with the bank, the family was later permitted to take possession of Beehive Cottage, a three-roomed gatelodge located near the upper gate to Killakee House. In the weeks preceding the re-possession of Killakee House, furniture and other household goods had been spirited away by locals only to reappear again in Beehive Cottage when the family had settled in there. Following the the eviction, the three Moran children were taken in and raised by Margaret Massy's family, the Leonards, at Meadsbrook Co. Meath

Hamon Massy had no income and no means of generating income. Other than his education at Harrow, he had no other qualifications. He was hopeless at managing his affairs, and he also had a chronic drink problem. His wife, as is so often the case in times of family crisis, quickly grasped the financial realities of their situation. She obtained a clerical post in the Irish Hospitals Sweepstakes in Ballsbridge, Dublin, and with her modest income she became the family breadwinner.

Death of Hugh Somerset, 7th Baron Massy

On 20th October 1926, Hamon's father, Hugh Somerset, 7th Baron Massy died, aged 62, at Ardfinnan House Co. Tipperary. He is buried with his wife in Ardfinnan churchyard. Hugh Somerset Massy appears to have been completely overwhelmed by the dramatic downturn in the family's financial circumstances. He spent most of his life, up the age of 51, in the shadow of his strong-willed father on whom he and his family were financially dependent. He lived the comfortable life of a country gentleman. He appears, however, to have had little or no involvement in the affairs of the Massy Estate up to the time of his father's death. From 1893 onwards his relationship with his father appears to have been a distant one.

All families experience periods of difficulty. From the time of the death of the 6th Baron Massy in 1915, however, the 7th Baron and his wife Lady Ellen Ida Massy had more than their share of problems. The squandering of the land settlement monies by his father, the sale of the family heirlooms, the burning of Hermitage, the loss of Killakee, the alcoholic addiction of their eldest son, the circumstances of his marriage, and finally the baptism of their grandson and heir as a Roman Catholic, all inevitably took their toll and must have contributed to their deaths at a relatively early age. The 7th Baron died intestate. From the time of the 6th Baron's death in 1915 to his own death in 1926 he witnessed the collapse of the family estate from a position of apparent great wealth to one of absolute penury. In the absence of a Will, administration of his estate fell to his eldest son Hugh Hamon, now the 8th Baron Massy. The Inland Revenue papers on file are incomplete in that the affidavit listing the 7th Baron's assets is missing. From the documentation on file, however, it is possible to determine that his personal estate was valued at £77-16s-0d. £67-16s-0d of this amount was comprised of outstanding and uncollectable rents from a number of smallholders in Co. Leitrim, thus leaving a net estate of £10, which passed to his eldest son Hugh Hamon Massy. It is also recorded by the Revenue assessor that at the time of the 7th Baron's death practically all the furniture in the house had been sold to meet everyday living costs. On the death of the 7th Baron, ownership of Ardfinnan House passed to his daughter Ida Lucy Massy, as stipulated in the will of his wife Lady Ellen Ida Massy. Ardfinnan House was sold to Mr. John English in 1928 and is still in the ownership of that family. Ida Lucy Massy died unmarried, in Irishtown, Clonmel, in 1957.

The 7th Baron's second son, Francis John Ingoldsby Tristram, married Evelyn Henry in 1920. He served as a Lieutenant in the Royal Fleet Auxiliary and died, aged 34, in 1929. His wife died in 1941. Their only child Cyril John Massy was born in 1925, served as a Lieutenant in the 8th Hussars, and died aged 22 in 1947.

Of the remaining two daughters, Muriel Olive married a Mr Keane and after his death lived in straitened circumstances with Ida Lucy in Clonmel, Co. Tipperary. She died in her late eighties around 1990. Lillian Ierne, was married firstly to a Mr King, and subsequently to a Mr Herbert Browne of Kenrick, Cumberland in 1929. She had one son, Anthony Massy Browne who lived in Wales.

The following obituary appeared in the Nationalist newspaper on 23rd October 1926:-

LORD MASSY

We regret to announce that Hugh Somerset John, Baron Massy, died on Wednesday at his residence, Ardfinnan House, Cahir, Co. Tipperary. He was the seventh holder of the title, which was created in 1776. He was born in February 1864, and succeeded his father, the sixth in the line, in 1915.

Lord Massy married in 1886 Ellen Ida Constance, daughter of Mr. Charles W. Wise, of Rochestown, Tipperary, by whom he had three sons and two daughters. The heir to the title and estate is the eldest son, the Hon. Hugh Hamon Charles George Massy, who was born in July, 1894, and married in 1919 Margaret, daughter of the late Mr Richard Leonard of Meadowbrook, Ashbourne, Co. Limerick.

Lord Massy had been a lieutenant in the Battalion of the Prince of Wales' Leinster Regiment.

The obituary is incorrect in that the 7th Baron had two sons and three daughters, and Richard Leonards address was Meadesbrook, Ashbourne, Co. Meath.

Hugh Hamon Charles George Massy, 8th Baron Massy of Duntrileague

Hugh Hamon Charles Massy succeeded to the Peerage on the death of his father in 1926. In material terms it was by now an empty inheritance. He became known as the penniless peer. His wife, Margaret, never used the title but referred to herself, and was referred to, as Mrs Massy.

The 8th Baron Massy never came to terms with the loss of his inheritance. He was unable to get employment, a fact that he attributed to employers being put

© *Massy (UK) Collection*

off by his title. It is more likely, however, that potential employers were aware of his alcohol addiction and of his inability to come to terms with the reality of his situation. For thirty-four years following his eviction he spent his time pottering about the Killakee Demesne and was regularly to be seen collecting timber for his kitchen fire in the nearby woods with the help of a boxcart that he made himself.

In 1936 Lord Massy was invited to the coronation of King George VI but he told correspondents at the time " *I have not enough money to take me to the nearest pub never mind to London for the Coronation.*"

On Friday 9th April 1937 the Irish Times published an interview with Lord Massy. In the interview, he spoke openly of his plight, and how his family depended on his wife's earning of 35/- per week to support them. He also told of how he spent most of his time in the deserted grounds of his former estate, and only visited Dublin about once a year. He was, he said, still being pursued by Leitrim County Council, for outstanding rates due on the family's former landholdings in that county. His chief interest now, he said, was his 16-year-old son Hugh Hamon John (Hughie), a student at Clongowes Wood College, whom he hoped might someday join the Navy.

Hamon Massy was a strikingly handsome man. The article was accompanied by a photograph of him, which graphically showed the deteriorating impact that his situation, and his addiction, had upon his health. By 1937, he was, quite clearly, a depressed and broken man, a shadow of his former self.

Demolition of Killakee House

The end of Killakee House came in 1941 when the bank, which had maintained a caretaker on the premises since 1924, and unable to find a purchaser, sold the house to a builder for salvage. Having removed the slates, roof timbers, floors and other saleable items, the builder demolished the house. It was an event that must have had a profound impact on Hamon Massy, occurring as it did in full sight of his little cottage. Although he had no alternative, living in the shadow of his former mansion was probably not helpful in putting the past behind him. The Killakee Woods were taken over by the Forestry Department. The demolition of Killakee House was a most unfortunate turn of events. Thousands of Ascendancy mansions were built in Ireland. Killakee House, however, both in its style and location, overlooking Dublin City and bay, was a house of particular merit. This aspect of the house was obviously noted by the bank, which paid a caretaker for 17 years to keep the house secure. In 1941, with the Second World War raging in Europe, it was evident to the bank that a buyer was not going to be found. It decided to cut its loses and sold the house for its salvage value. In 2001, sixty years after the event , Charles Guinness of Tibradden House recalled the demolition of Killakee House,

"In 1941, as a young boy, I walked up to Killakee with my mother when it was being demolished. The monkey-puzzle trees remained impressive and the huge glass-houses were still standing but vegetation had broken through the roofs. There was a melancholy atmosphere of decay and desolation. We salvaged a piece of stone and walked home sadly."

In 1946 Lord Massy was left £3,000 by a distant cousin and remarked, *"I don't remember him, but it was jolly kind of him to remember me".*

Around this time also Hamon Massy eventually secured casual work from a Mr Hans Veitch who had a charcoal-making business in the nearby woods. Despite his hopeless situation and his chronic drink problem, Hamon Massy had a polite and dignified manner, which was commented on by all those who knew or met him. He had a particular saying that he used in relation to the past glories of Killakee.

> **"If those trees could speak,**
> **and those mountains could see,**
> **many a tale you would hear."**

The 8th Baron Massy had a troubled and largely wasted life. He was incapable of managing his affairs and lived with his alcohol addiction for all of his life. One can only imagine how difficult it was for him to watch the decay of his magnificent estate (and his family's inheritance) literally before his eyes. There is a widely held, but mistaken, belief that the loss of Killakee House and Demesne was due to the alcoholism and poor money-management skills of the 8th Baron. This is not the case. The collapse of the Massy family's wealth can be directly attributed to the 6th Baron and his extravagant lifestyle. When upon his death the full facts of the family's appalling financial situation became known, continuation of the family's lifestyle became impossible. As the family had no means of income, bank debts grew alarmingly. The burning of Hermitage, and the non-payment of compensation, extinguished any possibility of even a modest financial outcome to the debacle. The family was in fact bankrupt. All of these things occurred before Hamon Massy succeeded to the peerage. The loss of Killakee was not caused by his personal failings. Indeed, it is more likely that the appalling sequence of events from 1915 to 1924, over which he had no control, exacerbated his personal problems.

Hugh Hamon Charles George, 8th Baron Massy died at Beehive Cottage on March 20th 1958, aged 63. In his will he stated " I desire to be buried in the ancient family vault in the churchyard at Castleconnell." The Will is signed 'Massy' and is, almost certainly, the last occasion on which the

baronial form of the signature was used. Following a funeral mass at the Church of the Annunciation in Rathfarnham, Dublin on 22nd March 1958, his remains were brought to Castleconnell and he was laid to rest in the Massy family vault in the churchyard attached to the Church of Ireland parish church. The journey from Killakee to Castleconnell is one that Hamon Massy would have taken many times in his youth as the Massy family moved back and forth between the two big houses. This last journey effectively marked the end of the baronial presence of the Massy family in Ireland. There is a certain irony in the fact that Hamon Massy, whose life was so terribly blighted by the collapse in the Massy family's wealth, should lie at rest in the family vault beside his grandfather, whose extravagant lifestyle was the primary cause of that collapse.

The following report appeared on the front page of the Evening Press of 21st March 1958:-

DEATH OF 8th BARON MASSY

The death occurred at his home in Co. Dublin yesterday of Hugh Hamon Charles George Massy, 8th Baron Massy, of Beehive Cottage, Rathfarnham. He was aged 64, and had been ill for some time. He is survived by his wife, Margaret, daughter of Richard Leonard, Meadesbrook, Ashbourne, a daughter Mrs. Brian Murtough; and his only son the Hon. Hugh Hamon John Somerset Massy (36) who now becomes the 9th Baron.

Descended from one of Ireland's oldest families, Lord Massy's barony was created in 1776. The family motto is "Pro Libertate Patriae" ("For the freedom of my Country"). The family had many Irish estates, the largest being Duntraleague Castle Co. Limerick, and Killakee House, Rathfarnham, Co. Dublin. Distress in the family fortunes over the years, however, resulted in Lord Massy, then the Hon. Hugh Hamon Massy, being evicted from Killakee House in 1924, at the suit of a Dublin bank.

The estate was taken over by the Land Commission, and during the Second World War the mansion was demolished. Lord Massy later returned to live in the three-roomed gate lodge "Beehive Cottage" where his wife served teas to Sunday trippers.

Left £3,000
Saying that he could not afford fuel, he used to cut wood twice a day, bringing it back to his cottage in an orange-box on wheels.

In 1946 he was left £3,000 by a cousin and remarked: " I don't remember him but it was jolly kind of him to remember me."

Lord Massy was educated at Harrow, and his son at Clongowes Wood College and Claymore School.

The report was accompanied by a photograph of the late Lord Massy in his younger years and a photograph of Killakee House.

Mrs. Margaret Massy

Hamon Massy had the great misfortune of developing a serious alcohol addiction at a young age and of inheriting a penniless peerage. He was, however, particularly fortunate in the woman he married. For the 39 years of their marriage Margaret Massy dealt with the difficult realities of their situation without visible complaint or recrimination. It was clear to all those who knew them that the bond between the couple was genuine and very close. Following the loss of Killakee she became the family breadwinner and by her efforts ensured that their life at Beehive Cottage was one of frugal comfort. In the late 1940s Mrs Massy

© *Massy (UK) Collection*

started a small tea-room at Beehive Cottage which opened at weekends. She was well known and liked by her neighbours, and was respected for the dignified manner in which she stood by and supported her husband throughout his difficult life. Without her loyalty and support, Hamon Massy's life, following the repossession of Killakee House, would undoubtedly have been even more tragic and short-lived. Mrs Margaret Massy lived on in Beehive Cottage for two years after her husband's death. In 1960 she moved to England where she shared her time between her daughter, Maureen and her son Hughie.

With her departure from Killakee, the last link between the immediate family of Lord Massy of Duntrileague and Ireland was severed 319 years after Captain Hugh Massy set foot in Ireland. Mrs Margaret Massy died, aged 78 years, at a nursing home in Leicester, England on 6th March 1971.

There are members of collateral branches of the Massy family still living in Ireland. Many more, however, have emigrated over the years to various parts of the world including the UK, New Zealand, Australia, South Africa, Canada and the United States.

Hugh Hamon John Somerset Massy

© *Massy (UK) Collection*

Hugh Hamon John Massy (Hughie), son of the 8th Baron and Mrs Margaret Massy, was born at Killakee House on June 11th 1921. He was the last Massy child to be born in one of the great Massy mansions. He was raised as a Roman Catholic and educated at the Jesuit College of Clongowes Wood, Co. Kildare. His mother's family and friends paid for his education. Although fully entitled to use the title 9th Baron Massy, he never did so. In 1941, at twenty years of age, he joined the British Army and served throughout the 2nd World War with the Royal Army Ordnance Corp seeing action at Dunkirk, North Africa and Palestine. On 18th September 1943 he married Margaret Flower of Barry, Co. Meath, who served with the A.T.C, and had four sons, David Hamon, John Hugh, Graham Ingoldsby and Paul Robert, and one daughter Sheelagh Marie. (For the first time in 300 years the eldest son of Lord Massy was not christened Hugh, a further break with the past.)

At the time of his father's death on March 29th 1958, Hughie Massy returned to Ireland to arrange the funeral and, interviewed by reporters at Beehive Cottage, said, *"I am going back to my wife and four sons in England. I have a business there and it is my job to look after it. There is nothing left for us here."*

His mother, Margaret, sitting by the fire in the tiny gate lodge which had been home to herself and her husband for thirty four years, said, " *All the land has been taken over by the Irish Land Commission. I think all we have left now is the gate lodge.*"

Beehive Cottage
© *The authors collection*

Although well aware of his ancestry, he seldom referred to it, and when he did it was without rancour or recrimination. His attitude to past events may well have been influenced by that of his mother. Those who knew him speak of a quiet-spoken, dignified and well-respected man who was at peace with himself and his life, and who held no resentment in regard to past events. Like his mother, he was primarily concerned with the realities of everyday living and with the future wellbeing of his family.

Hugh Hamon John Somerset Massy died in Cosby, Leicestershire, England on 5th August 1995, and is buried in the local graveyard. His children and grandchildren live outside of Ireland. They are ordinary people, leading ordinary lives. It would appear that the Massy family has finally achieved that level of relative anonymity that we all know as normality.

EPILOGUE

Hugh Hamon Charles, 8th Baron Massy (1894 - 1958)
and
Hugh Hamon John, 9th Baron Massy (1921 - 1995)
at Beehive Cottage Killakee (circa 1947)

Here traveller, scholar, poet, take your stand
When all those rooms and passages are gone
When nettles wave upon a shapeless mound
And saplings root among the broken stone,
And dedicate.... a moment's memory........

William Butler Yeats

Duntrileague Today

Lord Massy moved his residence from Duntrileague around 1790, and after an initial period in Massy Lodge, moved to Hermitage, Castleconnell in 1807. Nothing remains of the Massy house at Duntrileague. The family, however, retained ownership of the Duntrileague land for some considerable time. Of the church built by Hugh Massy II at Duntrileague only a ruined tower, under which he is buried, remains. The Charnel House, containing the remains of twenty-six Massy family members who died between 1811 and 1930, is basically intact but in need of some remedial work. For some years in the 1970s a hole in the structure enabled people to gain entry, but volunteers repaired this in the 1980s.

The following is a list of the persons interred in the Duntrileague Charnel House:-

Elizabeth Massy, relict of Hon. Eyre Massy, ... 25.02.1811
Charles Massy, son of Rev William Massy of Clonbeg, ... 03.06.1812
Hugh, 3rd Lord Baron Massy, ... 20.06.1812
Catherine Massy, wife of Rev. William Massy Jnr., ... 28.10.1813
Hugh Massy, Esq. of Riversdale, ... 07.03.1814
Hon. James Massy of Massy Park, ... 09.08.1815
Lucinda Massy, wife of George Massy of Glanwilliam, ... 17.03.1818
George Massy, son of George Massy of Glanwilliam, ... 12.09.1819
John Massy, son of George Massy of Glanwilliam, ... 13.09.1819
Constance Massy, daughter of late Hugh Massy of Stagdale, 14.03.1820
Rev. Godfrey Massy, ... 22.01.1831
Mrs William Massy, wife of Hon. William Massy of Belmont, 05.03.1831
William Nassau Massy, of Mitchelstown,
son of late Nassau Massy, ... 26.06.1835
Hon. Willliam Massy of Belmont, ... 11.09.1835
Infant son of Lord Clarina of Elm Park, Limerick, ... 02.10.1833
Rev. William Massy, Tipperary, ... 15.11.1833
Hugh Massy of Ballinacurra House, aged 84yrs, ... 03.03.1881

Charles William Massy of Grantstown, Co. Tipperary, ...14.10.1881
George Eyre Massy of Riversdale, ...30.04.1885
Robert Harding Massy of Ballygarrett, Mallow, Co. Cork. . .24.12.1886
Hugh Massy of Cregane, Buttivant, Co. Cork. 09.08.1887
John Massy of Kingswell, Co. Tipperary 03.05.1894
Lady Isabella Massy (Relict of 5th Baron),
Cambridge Tce, Paddington London. 27.07.1917
Hugh Hamon George Massy of Riversdale, ...22.04.1918
William Henry Massy-Bennett of Glenefy, ...09.06.1920
Hortense Mary Massy (nee Pennefather)
relict of Hugh Massy of Riversdale. 21.05.1930

Massy Lodge

Massy Lodge remains in the ownership of the Hanly family.

Ardfinnan House

Ardfinnan house remains in the ownership of the English family

The Massy Demesne at Hermitage – post 1920

Following the burning of Hermitage in 1920, and the non-payment of
compensation, the demesne of some 150 acres was sold in an effort to
address the Massy family's rapidly deteriorating financial situation. It
was acquired by a Mr William Moran. The burnt-out shell of the great
house stood until the mid-nineteen seventies when it was demolished.
Nothing now remains of the great mansion which once stood so
majestically on the banks of the River Shannon. The Moran family still
owns the land and a modern bungalow stands on the site of the great
house. A stone sundial in the front garden of the bungalow is the only
remaining artefact from the big house. The local Church of Ireland parish
church at Castleconnell contains many memorial plaques recalling the
Massy family's long association with the area. A Massy family burial
vault is located in the church graveyard. This vault contains the remains
of Lady Matilda Massy (nee White), wife of the 4th Baron; John Thomas

Massy, 6th Baron; his wife Lady Lucy Maria Massy; Hugh Hamon Massy, 8th Baron; and Edward Massy a distant cousin of the 6th Baron who died at Hermitage.

The Massy Demesne at Killakee - post 1924

Following its repossession, Killakee House remained unoccupied except for a caretaker, Edmund Burke, appointed by the bank. Nothing now remains above ground of the beautiful Killakee House, although some of the basement passageways can still be accessed. On close examination of the site one can also locate remnants of the great fountain and other garden ornaments. The upper entrance gateway and Beehive Cottage are still to be seen, as is the main gateway and gate lodge at the Rockbrook/Cruagh entrance to the demesne. A stone cottage on the Cruagh Road, at the upper end of the demesne, was once the gamekeeper, Somerville's, house and is still lived in by his descendants. The beautiful walled gardens created by Samuel White are in a state of total dereliction with no visible evidence of their former glory. Part of the foundations of the magnificent Turner conservatories can still be seen. The conservatories themselves are long since gone through a combination of neglect and vandalism. The gardens at Killakee were among the finest gardens of their type anywhere. The curvilinear conservatories were considered to be among the best of Richard Turner's masterpieces. Had the gardens survived, they would undoubtedly be regarded as a national treasure and placed in State care. However, what is gone is gone, and all that we have left are some old faded photographs that, nonetheless, clearly show the magnificence of what has been lost. A walk through the demesne reveals other features including some beautiful bridges over the Owendoher River, an ice-house and a filter mechanism for the water supply to the gardens. Part of the original *"Military Road"*, built by the British in 1803, following the 1798 rising, to enable troops to gain speedy access to the Wicklow Mountains, runs through the demesne. The building of the Military Road was the first application of civil engineering to upland roads in Ireland. Approximately one kilometre uphill from the Killakee House site, near a sharp bend in the road, is a reservoir that was constructed to supply water to the demesne. A network of underground cast-iron pipes ran from this reservoir to Killakee House, the Stewards House, stables, various small houses on the demesne and to the large fountain on the front lawn. Some of this piping still remains in functioning order. A small ruined stone house beside the reservoir is currently being restored by a local man Mr. Brian Quinn. On a hillside just above the reservoir is a large icehouse. Apart from Killakee House and gardens, the crowning glory of the estate was the beautiful woods. Thankfully, the woods are still substantially intact and in the care of 'Coillte' the Forestry Service, which has done some remedial work in recent years in association with a group called *The Friends of Massy Woods*, to restore the woods to their former glory and develop a number of nature trails. The woods are frequented by growing numbers of walkers and families, few of whom have any knowledge of the history of the Whites or the Massys.

IRA Bunker at Killakee

Early in May 1931 Killakee House was rented from the bank by the Detective Unit of the Dublin Metropolitan Division of the Garda Siochána for what was described as a 'hill fortress' to combat irregular military activities. There had been growing concern for some time about irregular subversive activities in the Dublin/ Wicklow Mountains. On the night of 23rd April 1931 Rupert Young, a Trinity student had been shot while walking near the Hell Fire Club with a friend. Young was hit by two bullets, one of which inflicted a face wound. On 10th June 1931 a massive explosives dump was found at Killakee in a concrete bunker buried in an overhanging bank of the Owendoher River (Abhainn Dughar, a branch of the Dughar or Dodder River), which flows through the estate. It contained rifles, revolvers, Lewis guns, thousands of rounds of ammunition and a large quantity of explosives, and was protected by a booby trap. The dump consisted of a bunker chamber about twenty-foot square and also contained a tent and bedding, as well as a supply of tinned foodstuffs. It was well constructed and spotlessly clean, the concrete walls being whitewashed and the wooden floor covered with linoleum. The roof was zinc-treated and cork lined to absorb moisture.

Overhanging shrubbery screened a small window in the side of the bunker. Entry was through a trapdoor that was well hidden. There was a second trapdoor inside, which could be closed to prevent light from the inside lamps being seen. The approach to the bunker was by way of the river, thereby concealing the footprints of those accessing it.

The arms dump was found by accident. One of the detectives from Killakee House sat down to rest on a rock beside the river and observed an iron pipe beneath it, which was later found to be a ventilation pipe for a stove. A thorough search of the area uncovered the doorway, which was so well concealed that it resembled a natural rock formation. It was suspected that the door was booby-trapped, so it was eventually opened by means of a long rope. A trap-mine was found at the bottom of the inner stairs, wired to explode if anybody walked into a tripwire located on the stairs. The dump was blown up by the army, the explosion being heard in the city. Three brothers were subsequently arrested and charged under the Treasonable Offences and the Firearms Acts.

Beehive Cottage

Following Mrs. Massy's departure in 1960, Beehive Cottage was purchased by a Mr Nicholas O'Brien, a retired Garda Superintendent, and his wife Margaret. It is still in the ownership of the O'Brien family and is maintained in beautiful condition.

The Stewards House

Across the roadway from the site of Killakee House are the Stewards House and Stables. This House was built around 1765 by the Conolly family of Castletown as a hunting lodge. It was they who also built the infamous Hellfire Club on nearby Mount Pelier. Luke White bought the hunting lodge and the Killakee lands from the Conolly family. During the 6th Barons tenure the house was the residence of his steward, Maurice Fox. Following the loss of Killakee House in 1924, ownership of the StewardsHouse passed to Miss Margaret Fox, his daughter. In 1968 the complex was purchased by the O'Briens and developed as an Arts Centre and tea-rooms. On April 29th 1970, Dublin newspapers reported that Mrs. O'Brien, who had just spent two nights on her own in the house, had been terrified by noises each night, and had discovered a great deal of damage throughout the house despite no evidence of a break-in. The O'Briens had experienced a number of mysterious happenings in the house since they moved in, in 1968. Workmen, whom the O'Brien's hired to undertake alterations, refused to stay in the house because of "ghostly" happenings. The Stewards House has, since then, changed ownership a number of times and was, until recently, a restaurant.

Lareen – Post 1912

Having acquired Lareen from the 6th Baron Massy in 1912, Mr Blacker Douglas used it as a sporting estate. On his death, Lareen passed to his second son, Charles. Charles kept Lareen until 1926, when he sold the house, lands and fishing rights on the Drowes River to Maxwell Boyle. Lareen House burned down in 1933, and four years later, Boyle sold the estate and fishery to Mrs. Sarah Hamilton of the Hamilton Hotel, Bundoran. It was bought in 1965 by Lareen Sporting Estates Ltd and Tunny Hotels. Finally, in 1977, the estate and fisheries were bought by Thomas and Betty Gallagher of Edenville. Since then Thomas Gallagher has developed the Drowes fishery, which regularly yields the first salmon of the season. The lands of Lareen now contain a number of houses which accommodate visiting anglers.

BIBLIOGRAPHY

The following is a list of publications and other documents which were consulted in the compilation of this book:-

Dunham-Massey Hall and Demesne History.
The National Trust of England.
Lodge, Peerage of Ireland, Vol. VII (1799)
Debretts Illustrated Peerage (1990)
The Complete Peerage, GEC, Vol. V111,-
Doubleday & Howard de Waldren
Burke's Peerage and Baronetage. 106th Edition Vol. II
Burke's Peerage and Baronetage. 1949 Edition Vol. I
Burke's Irish Family Records (Len-Z, 1976)
Book of Surveys and Distribution - National Library of Ireland (NLI)
Cromwellian Settlements in Co. Limerick, –
Limerick Field Journal Vol. 3.
Civil Survey 1654 - 1653 Vol. 4 (NLI)
Irish Record Sources for Family & Local History. James G. Ryan.
Commercial Directory of Ireland. J.Pigot (1820)
National Commercial Directory of Ireland. Slater 1846
Directory of the City & County of Limerick. G.H. Bassett (1889)
Great Landowners of Great Britain & Ireland. John Bateman (1879)
Index of Biographical Notices in Limerick Newspapers up to 1821 (NLI)
The Rise and Fall of the Irish Nation. Jonah Barrington (1833)
The Closing of the Irish Parliament. J. Roche Ardell (1907)
Pedigree of Lord Massy (Private Publication, 1776)
Masses of Massys. Hugh Massy, Vermont USA, -
(Private Publication, 2001)
Griffith's Valuation (NLI)
The Landowners of Ireland. U.H. Hussey deBurgh (1878)
Register of Wills (National Archives)
Thoms Directories (various years) (NLI)
Census Returns 1901 &1911 (National Archives)
Bennett Sales Catalogues 1918- 1925 (NLI)

Register of Claims – Damage to Property Compensation Act 1923.
Index of Church Memorials & Gravestones.-
Genealogical Society of Ireland
The Curse of Cromwell. D M R Esson (1971)
Twilight of the Ascendancy, Mark Bence-Jones, Constable (1987)
Guide to Irish Country Houses. Mark Bence-Jones (1988)
Sources for the History of Landed Estates in Ireland.-
Terence Dooley (2000)
Decline of the Big House in Ireland. Terence Dooley (2001)
Catholic University Church, St. Stephen's Green Dublin, –
Marriage Register
The Gardeners' Chronicle and Agricultural Gazette (Dec 10, 1864).
Book imports from continental Europe in the late 18th century.-
Hugh Gough, Long Room 38 (1993)
Dublin's Trade in Books 1550 –1800. M. Pollard, -
Clarandon Press Oxford (1989)
6th Baron Massy's Game Register 1887-1915 (Private Collection)
Hermitage Fisheries Register 1906-1928 (Private Collection)
A History of St John's Hospital, Limerick. John F Devane, Dublin
University Press (1970)
Representative Body of Church of Ireland Library – various records
Bolton Library, Cashel, Co. Tipperary – various records
Church of Ireland Records Office, Clonmel/Cahir Co. Tipperary.
Behind the Scenes, Ernie Shepherd (1983).
The Land League Days in the Galtees, John Gallahue - The Galtees
Anthology (2002)
Ballyroan Public Library, Dublin.- Local History Collection
Stillorgan Public Library. various records
Kinlough Diary 794 –1999. (tinet.ie/~fmasters/diary).
Kinlough Landlords. (tinet.ie/~fmasters/landlords).

Newspapers:-

Irish Times; Irish Independent; Leitrim Observer; Freeman's Journal
The Nationalist; Limerick Leader; Limerick Chronicle; Evening Herald &
Evening Press.

SDCC Crest

*The Crest or Coat of Arms of South Dublin County
reflects the ancient history of the area,
its geographic features and the work of the Council.*

*The motto "Ag seo ár gCúram - This we hold in Trust"
is an admonition to value, to preserve and to develop
the economic, social, environmental,
cultural and heritage assets of the area.*

COMHAIRLE CHONTAE ÁTHA CLIATH THEAS
SOUTH DUBLIN COUNTY LIBRARIES

COUNTY LIBRARY, TOWN CENTRE, TALLAGHT
TO RENEW ANY ITEM TEL: 462 0073

Items should be returned on or before the last date below. Fines, as displayed in the Library, will be charged on overdue items.

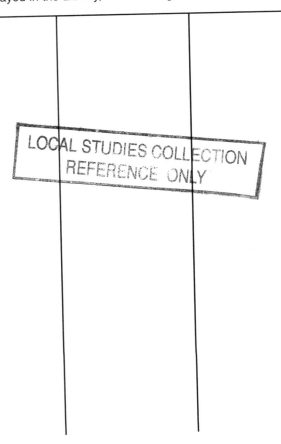